FOREWORD BY AM

IMPRINTED

Discovering & Parenting
Your Child's Identity

Leah ?
Shane

I bless
you to know
your 'I Am'

Tai Ann

TAI ANN MCCLENDON

IMPRINTED
Discovering & Parenting Your Child's Identity

Printed in the USA
ISBN (Print): 978-0-9908474-0-3
ISBN (Kindle): 978-0-9908474-1-0
ISBN (eBook): 978-0-9908474-2-7
Library of Congress Control Number: 2014951897

Prepared for Publication By

PALM TREE
PUBLICATIONS

Palm Tree Publications is a Division of Palm Tree Productions
www.palmtreeproductions.com
PO BOX 122 | KELLER, TX | 76244

Published by: KingShip Momentum, LLC | Abilene, TX

Unless otherwise noted, scripture has been taken from the New King James Version (NKJV) of the Bible. Copyright © 1982 by Thomas Nelson, Inc. Used by permission. All rights reserved.

To Contact the Author:

WWW.TAIANN.TV

DEDICATION

To my butterfly jewel,
my tender-hearted warrior,
and my smiling rainbow—
you are my truest treasures.
I love you with all my heart, all the time.

WHAT OTHERS ARE SAYING
ABOUT IMPRINTED

"Our actions, not our words are what truly count. Children grow up to become what they see each day, not what they are told to become. *Imprinted* will make it much easier to become that role model you wish to be."

—JIM FAY

Co-author of Parenting With Love and Logic | www.loveandlogic.com

"Tai Ann has discovered something powerful. The Bible refers to your children as arrows in your quiver. Your children are arrows you shape and fire into the future. Through them you have personally impacted the world. Susanna Wesley understood this as she shaped her little boys John and Charles Wesley. With this book you will also understand this sacred art."

—LANCE WALLNAU

President, Lance Learning Group | www.lancewallnau.com

"Each child is born with a unique identity—an imprint of the D.N.A. of God. Our charge as parents is to discover and develop our childrens' natural gifts, abilities, personality, and strengths. This must be embraced with intentionality if we are to see their true identities emerge and flourish unbruised. Delivered with warmth and humor, *Imprinted* provides you with practical tools to help you encourage your child's identity to thrive."

—WENDY K. WALTERS

Author of *Intentionality* and *Marketing Your Mind* | www.wendykwalters.com

"Tai Ann has been a valuable part of our community and church for a number of years, blessing many with her love and the wisdom she has gained as she has passionately pursued and lived for our Lord. It seems that often in conversation with her I gain something valuable for my life as a follower of Jesus, and I am certain this book will be the same."

—DAVID MCQUEEN

Senior Pastor | Beltway Park Baptist Church, Abilene, TX | www.beltway.org

"*Imprinted* is the kind of book that you make time for as a busy mother—especially when your greatest responsibility is helping to shape the identity of your children. Tai Ann McClendon gives practical, easy, and accessible treasures for any parent to pick up, try out in the home, and watch as their family transforms, blooming to life."

—CHRISTA BLACK GIFFORD

Author of *God Loves Ugly* | Speaker, Songwriter | www.christablack.com

CONTENTS

FOREWORD

As I began to read the manuscript *Imprinted*, I thought I knew a little of what to expect from a book about parenting. After all, I am a mother of two awesome grown children, and I studied Family Therapy. For the first decade of my practice as a licensed professional counselor, I specialized in working with children and teenagers, and my ministry continues to focus on the broken-hearted. I thought I knew what to expect ... I was pleasantly surprised.

I remember meeting Tai Ann for the first time—an amazing young woman of profound thought and speech who dreams big—and seeing the passion and fire that she carries for the Kingdom. I watched as Tai Ann and her husband, Paul, moved to our city to minister. The result of their pursuing God's identity and destiny is quite amazing and has brought breakthrough to many.

With great clarity and fun, Tai Ann takes that same Kingdom mindset into the actual parenting experience. Her application of the truths taught in this book make her stand out in a remarkable way. As I read her analogy of the sword in the chapter "Bless and Declare" I was moved to grab my own William Wallace sword. As

I held it before me, I visually received her teaching that to stop at blessing without making declarations makes for an incomplete weapon in the battle—instantly, I felt a shift within me to see victory in several of my own life's circumstances. Imagine if every parent who reads this book understands that they can fight for their child's identity NOW using the sword of blessing and declaring. Tai Ann carries great promise for each of her children and calls it out masterfully using her sword. You will love the stories that illustrate this.

Tai Ann makes family life an event and does it with great intentionality. Good parenting takes a lot of intention. I have heard it said that you either train your child intentionally or in your silence. Silence teaches our kids to fear what others think or wonder whether they measure up. "Fear of man" is a huge part of our culture and leads to ungodly peer pressure or pressure to conform to what is popular at the moment. You will see in these pages how Tai Ann is deliberate and purposeful while planting seeds and shaping the thoughts of her kids. Through the authority of parenting with "I Am" statements she found that a song is released as godly identity is realized in her children. She says, "The goal of 'I Am' statements is to strike the notes in your children's hearts so that they embrace themselves, embrace Jesus and play their song." As the song is released, the atmosphere changes and His Kingdom comes to earth. The ramification of this is huge in raising a new generation to change the world!

Every parent who reads this will be inspired by the victories that are shared in Tai Ann's stories, but also with the way she handles the situations where she admittedly didn't get it right. Even when her parenting is marked with frustration, she backs it with relationship, relationship, and more relationship. She has set a powerful standard to guide her kids and it is not based on her emotions. As parents we must never punish our kids for inconveniencing our lives. The story of Kai not wanting to get dressed during a frantic moment when the family needed to leave in order to be on time is a classic example of how Tai Ann lives this out.

As I read through the draft of this book, I expected stories and teachings that bring the Kingdom into the daily moments of a parent. Yet, it was so much more than that. I didn't know that I would cry and laugh and tell my husband over and over, "Listen to this: I wish I had this when I was a young mother and therapist!" It has a huge "wow factor" in every chapter and the fact that she is birthing this book in the midst of parenting her three young "kiddos" is courageous and brilliant. I quickly became excited realizing that many parents (and grandparents) will shortly be able to become equipped to make a real difference in the lives of their great treasures through the pages of this book.

It is with great joy that I commend to you both this book and my friend, Tai Ann. What you get is real, raw, and life-changing.

—AMY BLACK, MA, LPC

Regional Director of HeartSync Ministries
Founder of Undivided Heart, INC.

ACKNOWLEDGEMENTS

With more gratitude than a few words can express, I would like to honor and thank the following:

- ❖ Paul. You bring me such hope that the crazy ideas in my head can become a reality. Your undying confidence in me has kept me sane. You have listened to my thoughts more hours than any husband should. You have pushed me to risk, challenged me to action, and called me to live as a king. I cherish you.

- ❖ Mom and Dad. You have been so overwhelmingly consistent and supportive my entire life. Your belief in me has challenged me to believe as much. And at just the right time, you reminded me that what is within me needs to come out.

- ❖ Tanya Crump. Your love, revelation and impartation into my live is still making waves. I consistently come back to the foundations you helped me lay. "I Am" so grateful. You are a gift. In the truest sense, this is your legacy.

- ❖ Wendy Walters. You have a way of bringing the best to the surface. Your tireless effort and diligent work made this book a reality, but what I am most grateful for is the confidence you instilled in me and the friendship we've fostered. You lady, are good ground.

❖ Amber Holt, Lindsay Hood, and Amy Paquette. When I asked you to walk this journey with me, I knew the ease that would fall on this project. What I didn't expect was the treasure I would find in your random texts and constant support. You share in this inheritance.

INTRODUCTION

I am a mother. I have three adorable, crazy, life-giving kids. I hold a deep conviction that each child holds a unique display of the glory and wonder of the Lord. We, as parents, are called to help them find and cherish this greatness. It is with our molding, teaching, and loving that we imprint them as they grow. This can be haphazard or this can be intentional. Our goal is to intentionally imprint them with heaven's heart.

In the last decade, the Lord took me on a journey to discover who I truly am. He brought me wonderful mentors and great teachers. He taught me the importance of walking in my identity ... living free to be me.

When I became a mom, the idea of walking in identity began to unfold a new role for me. I longed to parent my children with the same tools that Jesus was teaching me to use as I walked into myself. I began to look at resources and listen to just about every podcast I could get my hands on. But when I started, resources on how to practically implement these ideas with children were few and far between. Everybody could agree that they wanted to raise children who knew their identity, but few were actually telling how they did it.

As my family grew, so did the amount of revelation the Holy Spirit deposited into my heart about how to creatively partner with Him in parenting. I knew that one day I wanted to bring these resources together into one place to help others who had the same desire to raise amazingly confident children that know who and whose they are.

When Jesus began to talk to me about this being the season to write, I honestly was hesitant. When you are writing a book on identity, people want to make sure the kids that you experimented on aren't crazy hoodlums living in the far country. They want to know that what you are talking about works. Most parenting books are written by people with grown children and grandchildren. This one isn't.

I am still a mother to young children. If you are looking for a book written by someone who has crossed the finish line, this is not it. I don't have the trophy of three awesome adult children to say that everything turns out okay. But what I do have is what Jesus told me—that He wanted me to write from the revelation of the season I was in, not from the memory of it.

So that is what I have done. These pages are filled with the revelations Jesus has brought me along my journey in parenting. They are life-giving and have already impacted my family immensely. I don't pretend to have all the answers, but I am willing to share my life and journey for His sake. I don't yet have grown children, but I have His promises to my heart and to my children. I have the testimonies of Him working on my children's behalf, in their world and in their heart. I have the memories of them embracing their identity and embracing Him, and I have peace that when I parent with Him, what we establish remains.

Before you read on, I'd like to introduce you to my family because you are going to hear a lot about them throughout this book. I am married to the love of my life, Paul. He has been my partner and my support. He loves crafting expressions of the glory of God. He walks as a priest and a king, and I love that God gave Him to me. Although this book is written with my heart and perspective, we are a team. We labor together for the sake of our children, and he is truly an amazing father.

We have three children. My oldest daughter is Adaiah. Adie is a true beauty and she loves everything princess. She has a creative heart and will usually be found coloring or drawing. She loves the feel of the wind on her face when she runs, and she unashamedly shares God's joy with those around her. She loves the idea of family and enjoys connecting with hers. She is quick to encourage and will often leave special notes just to let you know that she cares.

My middle child is my son, Kai. He is super-kind and loves to laugh and to have an adventure. He loves superheroes and is always up for a good game of Disney's Infinity. He walks in an incredible amount of confidence and security and will fight tooth and nail for what he feels is right. His biggest compliment to you is when he considers you a friend. He values friendship with everything inside of him, and he knows how to be a good friend.

My youngest is Zoe Kate. She will capture you with her smile and knows how to live life to the fullest. She adores Minnie Mouse almost as much as chocolate. She fancies playing dress-up and she wants to be where the action is. She loves playing outside but hates the cold. She is always rocking a good pair of shoes, especially some that sparkle. She calls herself a prayer princess and she thoroughly enjoys making your day brighter.

That's us, the McClendons, all of us. And don't worry, there won't be an addendum with more children. Our car and our hearts are full.

I wrote this book to help you discover and parent identity into your kids. Take what you find helpful and implement it. The revelation that Jesus has given me is not just for my family. It is also meant for yours. Seek heaven on behalf of your children and discover who Jesus made them to be.

Embrace your kids. Embrace yourself in the process. But most of all, embrace Jesus.

—TAI ANN MCCLENDON

July 2014

CHAPTER ONE

HARD-WIRED

It was a dark stormy night as we drove to my in-law's house. I was loving it because I thoroughly enjoy lightning storms. They remind me of Psalm 18 and how the Lord came down from on high to pull me out of the pit and rescue me. He came down with thunder and lightning because He delighted in me. Lightning storms always make me smile, reminding me how God loves and takes pleasure in me. My daughter Adie was about three, and afraid of the lightning flashing all around her. I began telling her about the lightnings of God, how they happened because He delights in her. She looked at me with such innocence and said, "Oh, you mean, these 'de-lights' are because He loves me and wants to show me?"

My mommy heart smiled and said, "Yep, that's it."

Her fear subsided, and we began to embrace the "de-lights" with excitement, commenting on their beauty. Even to this day in our family they are no longer referred to as lightning, but as the "de-lights."

Moments like these are the moments we live for in parenting, when what we are being intentional about connects deep in the heart of our kids. These are the moments that will last forever in our minds and in our hearts. It is no surprise to any of us that parenting is difficult and continually challenges us to grow and learn, but the joy of parenting lies in connecting with our kids—connecting them to themselves, and in them connecting to Jesus.

Hard-Wired for Greatness

Our children are hard-wired for greatness. They are made in the image of God. They are made with heaven's imprint on them. Children have untapped potential living inside of them, and they are made to be a glorious reflection of the One who's image they bear. As parents, our first job is to help them connect to their Creator. Second, we should help them identify and walk in the identity Jesus put in them.

Every child is hard-wired to reflect His glory. All of them are destined for glory. It is an individual imprint and will look different in every child. We learn about ourselves from our experiences, from others, and simple self-discovery, but the surest and truest way to identify our imprint is to go to the Creator Himself. As parents it is our responsibility to not only embrace our own imprint, but also to create atmospheres where our children discover and embrace theirs.

Embracing the reality that we are glorious because He is glorious is challenging. We are made in His image. This is not just a simple statement; it is a powerful reality that should be lived out with great confidence in each of us. We have spent much of our adult lives trying to figure out the imprint that lies within us—who we are and why we are here. How great a gift would it be to your child to help them identify their imprint while they are still young?

Christ has hidden treasures in each of our kids. When we take the time to find these treasures we honor the imprint of heaven in our children. We bring these treasures to the surface and show what we have found to our kids. We value what we uncover, and we keep the dirt and the soot off. It is our great pleasure to discover the gift of our children.

We are not meant to be mere men, we are meant to be the very vessels of God! We are the reflection of Him to this world. We are to exhibit His very nature and release it in and through our personal imprint. We are to share in the glory of the Lord Jesus Christ. When Christ came to restore He had us on His mind. He desired us to be brought back to our original intent. He desired us to be a true reflection of God … pure, holy, and glorious. When He sacrificed Himself it was more than to restore relationship, it was to restore our true nature.

There is a place in our hearts where we know this is true. Every child dreams of being someone influential or great. Girls dream of being a princess, boys dream of being super heroes. They dream of being the president, a fireman, a doctor, astronaut or teacher … but they never dream of being a bum on the street corner. They know they were created for greatness and their dreams reflect this knowledge. As parents we need to tap back into the innocent reality of our childhood—that we were created for significance—and even with our marred backgrounds we can still become a vessel of glory for the Lord.

No child dreams about being a bum on the street corner. They know they were created for greatness.

Focus on Identity

It is our job to raise our children so they live in and embrace their identity. When children embrace their identity, they naturally find their purpose. Identity begets destiny. To focus first on destiny will get you off course. To find identity will always lead to finding destiny. We know that the Lord has plans to prosper us, to give us a hope and a future. Let's step into our identity so we can partner with the future of the Lord within us. Only then can we teach our children how to embrace theirs so they can walk in their destiny as well.

My desire is to see a multi-generational group of people fully embracing their God-given identity, walking in fullness of their destiny, accomplishing all that Jesus set before them. I long to see individuals truly embrace the One True God and live in the fullness of His blessing. Understanding and embracing the cross will catapult us into the fullness He desires us to live in. It will cause us to be parents who lead our children into encounters with Jesus. We will teach them to embrace His grace and love, and walk with power indued from on high from the time they are young. I want us to be crowned with the love of Jesus, walking without shame and condemnation. Imagine families who resemble the family of heaven, loving one another into greatness!

This requires parenting with intentionality. It takes focus, but most of all it takes grace. We never want to parent out of performance or pressure. Our job is to impart love and identity into our babies. This happens when we give them what we have received from Jesus. We are not to give from a place of striving, but rather from a place of resting in Jesus and what He has done.

Purpose to be intentional and not to be reactive in parenting. Let's co-labor with God to imprint our children with the words of Jesus and the heart of the Father.

So where do we begin? How do we start? The simple answer is just start.

Begin talking to God about your children. He is the expert on them and He trusted them to you. To gain wisdom and insight into your kids, just ask Him. Jesus left us a helper, the Holy Spirit. He will not leave us as orphans, but will lead us into all truth (John 14). He is faithful and will speak to you about your children—the truth about them—and help you be the parent you want to become.

I love to ask Jesus about my kids. I love when He talks to me about their demeanor, their personality, and their future. What He says sticks with me, and it guides me in parenting. He is my greatest asset. If you are pregnant, ask Him about who your child is to be. Ask Him what to name your child. Many times He will guide you. The Lord knits your little one together in your womb, and He will reveal to you what He is creating.

What's in a Name?

I experienced a difficult labor when my third child was born. We had spoken to the Lord about her during pregnancy and decided on the name Zoe Kate, meaning "pure life." When she struggled inside my womb, I told her, "Zoe Kate, it's going to be okay. We are for you and so is Jesus."

In the midst of that labor when she was fighting to get enough oxygen, the Lord gently spoke to my heart that every time I spoke to her, I was proclaiming the very nature of her name over her. I was prophesying life over her when she needed it.

Names are important. Even if you have already named your child, ask the Lord why you were drawn to the name you chose. Find out what it means and seek God how it relates to their identity. There is power in a name. Let Jesus speak to you about the names of your children.

Deliberate Foundations

There are certain places where we can be deliberate in laying strong, secure foundations. Every person's spirit was created with specific needs:

❖ Every person needs to feel welcomed.

❖ Every person wants to feel valid.

❖ Every person needs to be accepted.

❖ Every person desires to be valued and loved.

❖ Every person craves security.

❖ Every person needs to know they have a purpose in this world.

❖ Every person was created to worship.

As our children navigate the waters of this world, we help them be prepared to fight off the storms and waves that would mar their understanding and keep them from walking securely on these foundations. To do this we must, and I mean must, be a consistent loving voice of truth to them. Teaching your children what Jesus says about these things while they are still young will help lay a firm, unshakable foundation of truth. Instead of having to go back and rebuild foundations in their adult life, they will be able to build mighty structures assembled on blocks of love and acceptance.

In 1 Chronicles 22:5, King David was dying and is talking to his advisors about the temple of the Lord. David said, *"My son Solomon is young and inexperienced, and the house to be built for the Lord should be of great magnificence and fame and splendor in the sight of all the nations. Therefore I will make preparations for it."* And that's exactly what he did. David made extensive preparations for the temple to be built before his death.

Now read 1 Corinthians 6:19: *"Or do you not know that your body is the temple of the Holy Spirit who is in you, whom you have from God, and you are not your own?"* When this verse was coupled with the one about David from 1 Chronicles it began to have very personal implications for me. These verses changed the standard for my life, convicting me to fully embrace the wonder of the Lord imprinted in me. I want to let His Spirit work in and through me to allow His glory to be made manifest in me, His temple—to be of great magnificence and fame and splendor in the sight of all the nations.

We are the temple of the Lord. We are designed to reflect the Lord in such a way that draws the world to Jesus. When we are faithful to emit His glory, He is raised up. And where He is raised up, He will draw all men unto Himself.

Our goal as believers is for the nations to submit to Christ. We are called in the great commission to disciple nations unto truth.

There is a simple reality that the power and presence of David's tabernacle continued for a season in Solomon's temple. We are to create a place that houses the power and presence of Jesus the way the tabernacle in the wilderness did, but it is also to have the glory, fame, and splendor which the temple had. It was not the tabernacle that the nations came to, it was the temple. The Queen of Sheba came to the temple noting its glory and splendor and remarking about the God it was dedicated to. If we want the nations to take notice of what is in us, we must merge the presence and the splendor.

Abundant Preparations

As parents we are to make abundant preparations just as David did. I have determined that even if I don't experience the level of splendor that will draw the nations, I will parent and prepare my children in such a way that they will be ready to embrace their call. We are truly entering a time of great wonder, and the Lord is looking to pour out His grace upon a people wholly submitted to Him, walking in their identity, and embracing His Spirit. We are chosen to raise up a generation that will literally affect the entire world for the sake of His glory. We have a wonderful call before us as parents. We get to show our children how He has made them glorious, how He has made them magnificent. We get to partner with the imprint of heaven so that they are made famous for the sake of His ways in the earth.

It may feel weighty, and it is. But the incredible companion to a significant call is the impartation to succeed. Weighty does not mean heavy. Remember His yoke is easy and His burden is light. Jesus has everything you need to be intentional in your parenting.

It is not you alone. It is you and it is Him. He will never leave you or forsake you. Your children will be taught by the Lord (Isaiah 54). You teach and He teaches. It is truly you co-laboring with God to raise your children.

I want to:

❖ encourage you to help your child find and walk in their identity;

❖ release tools you can use on a regular basis;

❖ empower you to partner with the Holy Spirit in uncovering the imprint of heaven in your children;

❖ teach you how to be the loudest and most consistent voice in their ears outside of Jesus; and

❖ show you how to recognize spontaneous, teachable moments and how to embrace them.

Psalm 8:2 says that through the praises of children and infants He establishes his stronghold against the enemy. Let's purpose to teach our children the fear of the Lord. Let's engage Jesus in the rearing of our children. Let's discover their hard-wire, and let's imprint them with heaven's words for their heart!

CHAPTER TWO

BLESS AND DECLARE

We are called to wield our weapon for our children. We are called to swing our swords. We are called to speak to their spirits and into their hearts. We are called to speak over their world and over their situations. We are and always will be a voice of truth to them and over them.

I love swords. I love their symbolism and I love the way they look. I love movies where swords are the primary battle weapon. I love the way they sound whooshing through the air. I just love swords. So it is no surprise that Jesus would speak to me with swords. When He asked me to be the vessel that spoke life over my children, He showed me a sword. He began to talk to me about how He has made my mouth to be like a sharpened sword, wielding the words of the Lord. My sword has two sides. One side is speaking blessing. The other side is declaring.

We are called to speak blessings and life. We can do this over ourselves and we can do this over others, but speaking blessing is just one edge of our sword. We are also called to make declarations over our circumstances and over our world. We need both sides of the sword. Without each side—blessing **and** declaring—the sword is incomplete, only half a weapon. We are to have a voice of influence over our children's spirits and over their world.

The Promise of Blessing

After the Father created Adam and Eve, the Bible says He blessed them (Genesis 1:28). Then He proceeded to declare into their world. If this is how the Father responds to what He created, then I want to do the same. I want to bless and I want to declare.

Blessing ourselves is a practice that has tremendous fruit. Bless is a word we take for granted and say regularly without any real thought about its meaning. "Bless you!" is an automatic response after someone sneezes, little more than an afterthought. We know being blessed is desirable, but we need to align our intentionality with blessing. By definition, to bless means *to invoke divine favor upon; to ask God to look favorably upon.* That alone should intrigue you to begin to practice this.

The history of the word bless comes from the Old English word, *bledsianē* based on *blood.* Its original meaning is *to mark or consecrate with blood.* This was influenced by the Latin translation, benedicere which means *to praise, worship* and later by association with the word *bliss.*[1]

What meaning contained in a single word! When you bless someone you are invoking the favor of the Lord. You are marking or consecrating them with blood. You are blessing them to praise and worship, and to experience bliss! This is not a casual word in our language. This is a powerful word—a commanding force, and a potent habit.

When you take the time to bless someone, you are taking the time to cover them in favor. When you do this with your children, you are inviting Jesus to breathe upon them and their character. I bless my children's hearts. I bless their minds. I bless their spirits. I bless their bodies. When you take the time to bless someone intentionally, you take the time to invite an experience with the favor of Jesus. An invitation with Jesus' favor is an invitation with Him.

Jesus received the little children. He took them into His arms and He blessed them (Mark 10:15-16). This is my favorite way to bless my children. I love to have them hop up into my lap and begin to speak tenderly into their hearts and their spirits. I love to bless their development. I love to bless them with joy and peace. I love to bless them with all the fruits of the Spirit. Most of all, I love to bless them with encounters with heaven and with God.

The Power of Declaring

Declarations are equally important. They are formal announcements of what you are aligning with. They help you align with faith, and they literally hold within them the power to create the things you are speaking. *"You will also declare a thing, and it will be established for you; so light will shine on your ways"* (Job 22:28 NKJV). God moves on our behalf when we make declarations.

Our words hold power. We hold the power of life and death on our tongues. When holding our most precious treasures, our kiddos, we must, and I mean must, watch our tongues. We need to foster the discipline to speak life over them.

Blessing and declaring over them is just one way you can do this, but regardless of whether you are intentional or not, your children hang on your every word. Be bold. Form their world with your words. Form their character with your blessings. Pick them up and hold them in your arms and speak tenderly to them. Verbally pour out your love, lavish it on them.

> **Your children hang on your every word. You form their world with your words.**

There are many different ways you can engage blessing and declaring over your children. How your personality functions may determine the best place for you to start. However you decide to move forward, just decide to move. It is for their benefit, and in the process you will be surprised at the way your heart connects to theirs.

One of my favorite ways to bless and declare is to take a scripture that is on my heart and turn it into a prayer over my kids. Let's use Psalm 92:1-3 (NIV): *"It is good to praise the Lord and make music to Your name, O Most High, to proclaim Your love in the morning and Your faithfulness at night, to the music of the ten-stringed lyre and the melody of the harp."*

I take the scripture and turn into a personal blessing like this:

"Kai, I bless you in the name of Jesus. I bless your heart to enjoy the presence of the Lord. I bless your spirit to connect to Him in ways that make you acquainted with His love and His faithfulness. I bless you to find wonder in His ways.

"Kai, I declare that you will rise up to worship. I declare that songs of praise will be in your heart and will surround you. I declare your spirit to wake up to the places that you are to make music unto the Lord. I declare moments to find you where you have the opportunity to learn to praise Him."

Scripture is our Secret Weapon

Scripture is powerful. When we use scripture as a weapon of warfare, we become powerful. Our prayers carry a weight backed with 2,000 years of history. We are aligning our children with the very Word of God.

Bless and declare prayers can be lengthy or they can be short. Both are powerful because both are blessing who they are and declaring over their world. Consider Proverbs 19:11: "*A man's wisdom gives him patience; it is to his glory to overlook an offense.*"

This scripture is the basis for a simple prayer I declare over my kids when they are grumpy with each other. It goes like this:

"Adaiah, I bless your spirit to be in tune with God's wisdom and to receive patience from it. I declare that you have the ability to overlook everything that is annoying and frustrating you and the wisdom to know how to extend grace."

Here is one more example for good measure. In 1 Samuel 3 the Lord spoke to young Samuel during a time when hearing the Word of the Lord was rare. Eli was the priest, and Samuel worked under him. Samuel kept hearing the Lord speak, but thought it was Eli. Eventually Eli recognized what was happening, and directed Samuel to respond to the Lord, ready to listen. From this scripture I speak this prayer of blessing and declaration:

"Zoe, I bless your spirit to connect with the Holy Spirit. I bless you to recognize the sound of His voice. I bless you to be sensitive to the subtle ways that He moves, and to recognize the bold moves He makes on your behalf. I bless you to walk in this from a young age.

"Zoe, I declare that you will have people of God surrounding you your entire life. I declare that they will know the voice of God and will be able to help you connect with your Maker. I declare that you will heed wise counsel and will walk in obedience to what God is speaking to you. I declare that you will have confidence in the words of the Lord to you and that it will shape a future where you can be used in mighty ways."

Crafting "bless and declares" is something I have practiced and becomes easier the more I do it. Don't be discouraged if you are just beginning. The point is to begin to speak life. One of my friends and intercessors, Amy, started by writing a blessing prayer that she could read over her children regularly. It was a way she could begin to speak life over her children with a piece of paper in her hand. It built her confidence as she was trying something new and learning a new way of thinking and praying. Remember, it doesn't matter the method you use, the point is to be intentional with your words over your children. Amy desired to be able to bless them from head to toe as she was putting them to sleep. Here is her prayer:

"Child, I call your spirit forth in the name of Jesus. I bless you to receive all the love God has for you. To be filled to the measure of the fullness of God. I bless your mind. You have the mind of Christ. I bless your eyes to see and your ears to hear the things of Heaven. I bless your nose to smell the fragrance of Heaven, and I bless your mouth to speak life and not death and to taste and see that the Lord is good. I bless your arms and hands to be kind and generous and to do the work that God has prepared in advance for you to do. "

I bless all the organs in your body to work exactly as Father designed them to work. I bless your legs and feet to be strong and straight and to carry you to many places to share the Gospel of peace. I bless your heart to be a heart of purity because the pure in heart will see God. I bless you to rest in His arms as you sleep tonight and to have dreams of your destiny in His Kingdom, to have visions and Angelic visitations.

Your words are powerful. The Father created the world with words. You are made in His image and have the wonderful ability to speak. You words create—they just do. Regardless if you focus them or not, your words create your world. Submit your tongue and your words to the Holy Spirit and bring intentionality into the picture. When you do, you will be bridled with a tongue that creates life for your children.

As parents we know there are just days when your toddler seems to throw a fit every minute of the waking day, or your elementary kid comes home displaying attitudes and words that you know they didn't learn at home. There are days when your potty-trained three year old decides that the potty is no longer something they want to use. We all have these moments where we know our children are dealing with more than they can communicate to us. We know the way they are behaving isn't who they are or their typical practice. It is on these days that I put them to bed, wait until they fall asleep, and then go back in to pray over them.

These are the times I go sit down on their bed and I speak boldly. I call their little bodies and spirits back into kingdom alignment. I declare that the enemy can't pervert who my child is going to be, and I bless them to commune with the Father in their dreams. I declare Psalm 16:5-8 over them. I declare that they are not alone and that they are secure. I declare the Lord's boundaries over them. I bless them to hear the counsel of the Lord, even while they sleep. I bless them to wake up with their eyes on Him, refreshed and ready to enjoy life.

Never underestimate the power of a parent who wields their weapon on behalf of their child. And when you don't feel like you have what it takes, remember that the Father will wield His sword on your behalf. You're His precious child, and He will speak tenderly to you about who you are— blessing you, and speaking life over your world. Receive from Him and then be willing to replicate that grace.

Never understimate the power of a parent who wields their weapon on behalf of their child.

Endnote:

1. *New Oxford American Dictionary, 2nd Edition.* 2005. New York. Oxford University Press.

CHAPTER THREE

I AM STATEMENTS

*For you did not receive the spirit of bondage again
to fear, but you received the Spirit of adoption
by whom we cry out, "Abba, Father."*

—ROMANS 8:15 (NKJV)

"What's Your last name? If I am Your child, adopted into Your family, I need to know my new last name."

My mentor, Tanya, began to ask this of the Lord. Such a simple question, but such an important one. As the truth of her sonship began to hit home, her curiosity wanted an answer to this question. What was the imprint of the Father's family that was upon her? Adoption is a legal transaction. Every time it occurs, the name of the child being adopted is changed to match that of the family. So Tanya wanted to know what the identity was that was being attached to the discovery of her adoption.

The Lord gave her a gracious encounter where He took her to Exodus 3 when Moses asks about his own personal identity.

Instead of answering Moses about his identity, God answers about His own. *"I Am who I Am."* As the passage goes on, God declares that this is the name that is to be passed from generation to generation. **I Am** is God's generational name.

Your last name is your generational name. It is the name you pass to your children, and the name they will pass to their children. The generational name of the Lord is "I Am." You have been adopted into His family and you are branded by the **I Am**.

Oddly enough, there is not a culture or a people on earth who don't use the word "am" in some way. Am is the first person, singular form of the verb "to be." It means having the state, quality, identity, nature, or role that is specified. Each language does it differently, but each language has a way of claiming personal roles. Even in movies where language barriers are a hindrance to communication, people still find a way of stating who they are. I see the scenes where one person taps their chest and says their name, then the other person does the same. People find a way to claim their identity.

What Jesus began to reveal to us was two-fold:

❖ What we attribute with "I Am" needs to be a reflection of His character. We are made in His image and adopted into His family. We must begin to see ourselves that way and line up our identities and words to match.

❖ The way we truly find our identity is by knowing His. As we discover who He is to us, we discover who He is through us.

Let's take a simple look at it. "I am a failure." "I am too much." "I am afraid." "I am ugly." "I am lacking." None of these are accurate statements. None of them. Remember, you are made in the image of God. What you attribute to and link with the words "I Am" need to be a reflection of God. You are not a failure. It is not part of your state, design, or nature. You may feel like a failure, but a feeling is not attributed to your identity.

You are not too much. You may feel like too much, but you are made in the image of an infinite God who knows the right time for the right thing. This feeling is not part of your identity. You may feel afraid, but fear is not your identity. It is something that tries to keep you from who you are, but it is not who you are. You are not ugly. You may feel ugly, but it is not part of your state of being. You were made in the image of a glorious God. So how can ugly be part of His expression in you? You are not lacking. You may feel like you don't have capacity or capabilities to excel in an area, but you were made in the image of the One who is perfect and complete, lacking nothing.

This may seem like I am being picky about word choices, but it is much more than that. This is choosing to align yourself with His identity in you. This is choosing to let only His expression be your plumb line, the truthful and accurate one. A feeling is very different than owning something as part of you. Let's make sure what we own as part of us is truly who we are and who we are made to be.

Choose to align yourself with His identity in you.

"I Am Statements" carry weight and have a definitiveness to them. They have authority in them, and they change atmospheres. Ironically, when I am getting attacked in my identity, the question I find myself asking is, "Am I? Am I what I fear? Am I what the enemy is saying? Am I really like that?" This question undermines confidence and threatens identity. There is a lack of certainty in it, and it is laced with fear. When you begin to ask yourself the "Am I" question, go talk to Jesus. "Am I?" needs to be answered with an "I Am." The only place to find our "I Am" is with Him. It is who we are in Him and who He says we are that defines us.

"I Am" in You

Who God is to us is who God is through us. When we understand that He is the Healer, we understand that He has put healing in our hands. When we know Him as the Word of Life, we have a different capability to use our words to bring life. When we know God as Love, we can understand that we can love with a supernatural kind of love. Our deepest clarity is found only in Him. To look for our identity apart from Jesus will bring us a partial understanding, at best, of who we were made to be. There are plenty of resources in our day and age that press into the self-help, self-discovery world. They may bring a level of understanding of identity, but the fullest way to discover yourself is always found in looking at the One who you were made like. Remember you were made in His image, so looking at His identity will always reveal something about you.

In Matthew 16, Jesus asks the disciples who people say that He is. After giving various replies, Jesus then asks them who they say that He is. Simon responds that Jesus is the Messiah, the Son of the living God. Jesus then turns to Simon, speaks life over him and reveals his identity. He is now known as Peter, the rock.

It is in knowing who Jesus is that He tells you who you are. We are who we are because He is. When your identity flows from His, it takes off the pressure of performing. Your confidence ultimately lies in who He is to you and through you. He is the Great I Am. He is the One who is here today, present in your world. He is the same yesterday, today, and forever. We exist in this form because He is.

When I first began to use "I Am Statements," it began to revolutionize my world. There is something about hearing from heaven on who you are that changes you. Many people have bookmarks, notecards, or teachings found in scripture of the identities each of us share. These universal truths such as being a child of God, a daughter of the King, or a priest are helpful, but I love the personal expression in "I Am Statements." This exercise is fully personal to me or to the one whom I am speaking over. It happens by going to Jesus and hearing what He says about my identity. Each of us have been given different expressions of our Father God, and to receive "I Am Statements" that speak to those unique parts is freeing and empowering.

One of the first "I Ams" I received was that I was an arrow in His quiver. I was in college and desperately seeking identity. I was feeling unused and undefined. I was crying out for definition and longing to know I wasn't forgotten. My lack of clarity was beginning to make me hopeless. When Jesus spoke to my heart that I was an arrow in His quiver, it did something for me that went beyond just hearing who He was to me. It felt personal and it touched me in a way that other words hadn't. "**I am** an arrow in His quiver." The "I Am" resounded with the reflection of God in me. He told me He was sharpening my tip and making sure that when I was shot, I would fly straight. This spoke of Him as my archer. The One who knows where I am aimed, the One who loves me enough to make sure I hit my target. I began to take that word and war with it. I started a list of "I Am Statements" and I declared them over myself regularly. Having this personal word armed me to fight off the lies of the enemy that were causing hopelessness in that season.

"I Am Statements" are fascinating. Because they are connected with who He made you to be, they stir different things in different seasons. A friend prayed over me while I was stuck writing this book. She heard the Lord say, "Tai Ann is an arrow. She will fly straight and true and her words will pierce their mark because she is an arrow in His quiver." As soon as she spoke that word, it totally broke me. I was seen by the Lord. He was reminding me of His promise from years past. He was reminding me of my identity, and He was reminding me of who He was to me. When you declare your "I Am Statements" over yourself, you are inviting an encounter with that part of God. Being reminded that I was an arrow in His quiver brought me into an encounter with my Archer.

Parenting with "I Am"

So how do "I Am Statements" fit into parenting? At my house they are a regular practice. They have become one of the primary tools we use to embrace ourselves and to fight the lies of the enemy. When my first daughter was young, I began to ask the Lord to speak plainly about her identity. I was purposely seeking His words on who she was. The first "I Am Statement" He gave us was her name, Adaiah Joy. It means God's ornament, jewel, and witness of joy. I remember holding her in my arms when she was just days old, and feeling the nudging of the Lord to begin to speak her "I Ams" over her. I would look at her and speak to her spirit. I would tell her, "Adie, you are the Lord's witness of joy. You will know the joy of the Lord and it will be your strength. It will lead people to Him because of your joy for life."

I did this regularly and wrote down the new things that He would speak to me about her. I treasure the words that the Lord has given me for each of my children. I started affirming their identity by speaking gently to their spirits, even before they knew how to embrace it themselves.

Many of you have children beyond the infant years, and I want to make it plain that it is never too late to start speaking identity over them. It is never too late to stir their spirits with their personal imprint of heaven. You have authority to speak into your children and to remind them who they are to be.

> **You have authority to speak into your children and to remind them who they are to be.**

As my children grow, I teach them how to war for their own identity with "I Ams." Most nights when we go to bed and many days in the morning, we speak our personal "I Am Statements" over ourselves. Knowing your identity is one of the main things that will keep you anchored in truth. The earlier you know your true identity, the better. Most of us didn't really embrace ours until we were adults. Think about the kind of adults our children will become as they walk confidently, secure in their identity from an early age.

You train them to do this by having them simply repeat after you. For example, with my oldest I would say, "I AM a jewel of God." Then my daughter would repeat, "I AM a jewel of God." Then we would go on to the next one. We would always say our "I Ams" with unction, owning them. Any time one of the children doesn't fully own their "I Am" statement, I have them say it again. Remember there is empowerment in the "I Am" because it comes from the "Great I Am!"

I started this practice when they were first learning how to talk. Now that they know and own their "I Ams" they don't repeat after me any longer. They declare them by memory because they are written on their hearts. It has become something my kids look forward to so much that if I forget to do them, they ask. I once asked them why they enjoy them so much, and the honest response I got back from Adaiah was that it made her heart feel alive. Simple statement, but profoundly true. "I Am Statements" make your heart feel alive. They connect you with the deepest parts of you and to the deepest parts of Him.

When Adaiah was just three years old we had the opportunity to see how "I Am Statements" affected her view of herself. She was in a mother's day out class and came home one day talking about a boy who had called her poo-poo head. She was really upset by it. It had really affected her heart. I reminded her that she didn't have to receive those words. I asked her if it was true, and she quietly said, "No."

I asked her, "Who are you?" and she began to go through her "I Ams":

- ❖ "I AM God's witness of joy" (this is what her name means).

- ❖ "I AM momma's jewel."

- ❖ "I AM daddy's princess."

- ❖ "I AM graceful and kind ..." and so on and so forth.

The next day at school, I asked her if the little boy had said anything this time, and she said in a very happy tone, "Yes he did! He called me poo-poo head again."

I was kind of shocked by her excitement, so I asked her why she was so happy about it. Adaiah said, "I told him I didn't receive it because I was my daddy's princess!"

Adaiah knowing her identity kept her grounded in what was and wasn't true about her. She was only three years old, but knowing the truth about who she was, was extremely powerful and it moved this mama to tears.

Your "I Am" Song

I once asked the Lord what these statements really do. I heard this beautiful musical note. The Lord said that when an identity statement hits home, it resounds with your soul. This note rang true and loud. Then a few seconds later, I heard another note. It was different but equally as piercing and beautiful. Then came another, and another, and another ... all getting closer together and gaining momentum. A glorious song began to break out, one that I had never heard before. The Lord then told me when you connect with your identity, you are hitting the note of your song. The more you connect with it, the more notes you hit. As you begin to embrace yourself—your true self—your glorious song is played. It fills your being with life and it is played loudly enough to entice others to play their song too. The goal of "I Am Statements" is to strike the notes in your children's hearts so that they embrace themselves, embrace Jesus, and play their song.

I remember driving, doing errands, and Kai my son asked to do our "I Am Statements." So we start spouting off our favorites. Kai would give one, Adaiah would give one, then I would give one. All of a sudden my littlest, Zoe, began crying. I pressed into her and asked her why she was so sad. She was only about 17 months old at the time, so her reply was in very elemental words. She said, "I Yam. ME."

I had totally overlooked her in our fun. She was sad and feeling left out, but even deeper, the songs of our identity were causing her to want to embrace hers. So we all stopped and encouraged her to go. "I Yam Zoe!" "I Yam loved" "I Yam wife (life)!"

She jumped in with all of her energy and gave it all she had. There is something compelling about knowing who you are. It entices others to know the same.

My mentor, Tanya, gave me a picture that has never left me. She talked to me about how the identity and promises of the Lord can never fade. She described a bird's nest that was made by the enemy. He had gone and picked up twigs and leaves and was diligently making a place to sit. In the midst of this nest were red ribbons. Some of these red ribbons had promises on them. Some of them had statements of identity. All of this was intricately woven together with his lies, deceit, and wounds. The scene began to change. The Father grabbed the nest and began to carefully unravel the mess. He would set aside the twigs and leaves and lies. He was purposefully unweaving the tangled nest that held His promises and our identity captive.

This picture has always been reassuring to me. The promises of the Lord and our identity cannot be stolen. They are sealed with the blood of Jesus. They may have been a place where the enemy sat and spoke lies to us, but what the Lord intended can't be destroyed, only perverted and misused.

Many times we can't clearly see what the Lord put inside of us, but we can see the perversion of it. My Kai has always been a super sweet little guy. As long as I can remember, he has had a super tender little heart. So tender that at times he will get his feelings hurt over the tiniest things. I remember being bewildered that what was going on was hurting his feelings so much. One time when he was two years old, I remember him crying because I offered him a blue shirt and a red shirt to wear. The crocodile tears just poured down his face. Many times, I would get frustrated with his sensitivity, but today, I heard the Lord settle my soul. He prompted me to ask Kai, "Why are you so sad?"

He whispered back, "Because I really wanted to wear orange today."

Boy, I wasn't expecting that one! Much ado about nothing ... or so I thought. The Lord gently reminded me that he had made

Kai tender. So I put the orange shirt on Kai, and then sat down to vent to the Lord.

I wish I could say that this whole thing hadn't ruffled my feathers, but I was in a hurry that morning, and cuddling and helping his heart understand that I wasn't trying to limit him was not in the schedule. But when conviction and the voice of the Lord comes, you gotta adjust your schedule. I told the Lord that I didn't know how to handle this part of my sweet boy. The Lord then said, "I made him to be a tender-hearted warrior. One who wars for my heart to be known and one who feels for my people. Don't parent that sensitivity out of him."

I sat there in shocked silence. I had missed it. I had missed a precious gift that the Lord had given my son. What I thought was a lack of emotional development was really a gift. Kai is to be a compassionate, kind, and tender-hearted individual, just like Jesus. So later that day I sat down with Kai and apologized for trying to squish his feelings. I told him that he was made to feel deeply because he was a tender-hearted warrior. It was an "I Am Statement" that the Lord un-wove from the nest of the enemy that day. Now when those times of tenderness come, I parent them with understanding, and I can align with what Jesus said about him.

I sat there in shocked silence. I had missed it ...

Lots of times, when my kids are struggling with something, I will ask them what God would want in their character. We will all ask Jesus and then talk about what we are hearing. Once we hear, we make it an "I Am Statement." There was one day when Adaiah was struggling with her attitude. She was grumpy, and she was having no problem letting that grumpy out on everyone around her. So as we were driving in the car, we all stopped and listened for Adie. Her heart was so hard that she was just kinda going along with what we were doing. But Kai and Zoe jumped in. Zoe said Adie makes her happy. Kai said something similar. I had an "I Am Statement" dropped into my spirit for her. I said, "Adie, you were made to set and change atmospheres. What kind of atmosphere do you want to set in this car?"

"I don't know," she responded.

So I pushed a little more and asked her, "What kind of atmosphere does Jesus release?"

She said, "He releases joy … hey, my middle name is Joy! Maybe I can release joy too."

So I instructed her to put her hands on Kai and give him joy. She did and Kai started laughing. Then I told her to put her hands on Zoe and the same thing happened. I looked back at Adie, and she was smiling ear to ear, and said, "I Am an atmosphere setter!"

She had connected with a chord in her song, and it not only changed the atmosphere of her heart, but the atmosphere of the car.

One of the best ways to benefit from "I Am Statements" is to repeat them regularly over yourself. There is a YouTube video about this called "Jessica's Daily Affirmation." A little girl is standing on the bathroom counter affirming herself and her day. She had self-confidence and it only seemed to grow throughout the clip. There is something about affirming yourself that is catching. There are now more than 14 million views of this clip.

If you haven't seen it, go look it up. You will feel the power of speaking life and will find a smile on your face.

I would like you to start a list of the "I Am Statements" for you and your kids. Make sure it is in a safe place, and one that you can access regularly. You will find yourself identifying with and warring with certain statements for a season, and then the ones you use regularly may change. This does not mean they are no longer valid, it just means that you are looking at a different angle on the same jewel. We are each crafted as jewels of the Lord; we are multi-faceted and glorious. In different seasons, our jewel may be turned at a different angle, but our "I Am Statements" are still part of us, even if the light isn't shining on them at that moment. Embrace yourself. Embrace your children. Help them discover their identities and strike the notes of their unique song. As we do, they will wake up to themselves and find Jesus, the Great I Am!

CHAPTER FOUR

THE POWER OF CHOICE

Free will is a wonderful and amazing thing. The power of choice is a beautiful gift from God that makes our life full of meaning. What we choose can empower us or cause us setbacks. We can choose to believe a lie or the truth. We can choose to act out of our God-given identity, or we can choose to avoid it. Either way, our choices end up defining our lives.

Anyone who has been a parent knows what most children's favorite word is by fifteen months, "No!" They are realizing they have a choice and they want to make sure you know that they know! After a long day of battling with boundaries with my early walker, I remember thinking about when they were younger. Even though I was more tired then, I already missed the age where they just smiled and cooed. I have enjoyed every stage with my kids, but the reality of them waking up to their choice was overwhelming. So, how do you begin to parent choice?

Our world is becoming more and more full. Our children's generation will have access to more information than has ever before existed in the history of the world. They will have access to more technology, more entertainment, more options ... just more. It is important that we begin to teach them to make quality choices and train them how to make healthy ones. We must teach them about the power of agreement.

The Power of Agreement

As parents, it is our responsibility to teach our children how to align (come into agreement) with truth. Agreement is being in harmony in opinion or feeling. Everyone makes agreements with belief systems. Our desire is that our children make agreement with the belief systems that align with who they are and who the Lord is. This is not a one-time decision, it is a way of living ... a continual choosing. We must first help our children identify the places where a conscious choice is needed, then give them the tools necessary to make a good choice.

One of the most amazing scientific discoveries I have found was uncovered by scientists at Oxford University. They detected what they believe to be the seat of conscience, the lateral frontal pole. It is a study centered around the brain's connection with morality. The lateral frontal pole is the region of the brain that makes you wonder if you have done something wrong, and whether or not you would have been better off to do something different. One of the coolest things about this part of your brain (which is about the size of a brussel sprout) is that you have two different poles, located behind each eyebrow. It is unique only to humans, and it fascinates me. We have places specified in our brain that talk to us about good and bad and right and wrong. We have been given the ability to reason and to choose. We have been given a conscience that helps guide us. We are responsible for teaching our children to listen to their's and to act accordingly.

When talking about alignment, the obvious place to start is with the question, "What are you aligning with? " We want our children to align with their identity, but we are also parenting core values and beliefs into our children. If you aren't proactive about the values you choose to instill, the world will choose for you.

Choosing Your Family's Values

One of our family values is knowing Jesus. We want our children to be familiar with Him. We are not content for them to just know stories about Him, we want them to understand that they can experience Him, tangibly feel Him, hear His voice, and feel the Holy Spirit. My husband, Paul, and I have made sure that regardless of what else we do in our parenting, this is one value we hold on to. This may sound obvious for Christians, but we have made sure to be specific about not just telling about Jesus and our faith, but creating spaces for our children to engage their own faith, even at their early ages.

Another one of our family's values is forgiveness and connection. We are extremely deliberate about working through issues that cause our hearts to be disconnected. We know it is possible to maintain connection through the craziness of life. Issues are obviously going to arise, but if you make it a priority to work through the issues as they arise, you will guard and protect the thing that matters most in your family, your connection to each other. When my kids squabble, and they do, we make sure to fully finish an issue.

When I first got married to Paul, he made it abundantly clear that when we argued or disagreed, forgiveness was a priority. He told me about the difference between "I'm sorry," and "Will you forgive me?" I'm sorry does speak of regret, it is just not always clear what you are regretting. Is it the action that caused your hearts to separate, or is it the regret of getting caught? "Will you forgive me?" requires humility to ask, and it postures you in a place to regain connection.

When someone says, "I'm sorry," the other person usually responds with "It's okay." But is it? Are they? Usually not. It is a dismissive answer that simply acknowledges the matter. Forgiveness requires a choice. It is a choice to lay down the offense and move past it without carrying the issue forward any more.

When my kids get into disagreements, the way we work through issues is by addressing what actually happened. It typically requires identifying why something hurt someone's feelings. Then, it is up to the offender to offer an apology and ask for forgiveness. We do this often enough that my kids understand what this means. Now, if the offender is not ready to ask for forgiveness, we don't push it. But we talk about the loss of connection that their sibling will feel until the issue is fixed. This is where as a parent, I rely heavily on the conviction of the Holy Spirit. It never fails. The child who offended will come back and ask for forgiveness because they have realized that their actions have negatively impacted the family.

When our children were just toddlers we began to train them to ask for forgiveness. It is the verbiage and action that we have been convicted to hold as a core value. When they would go take a toy, hit another toddler, or say something tacky, we choose not to say "I'm sorry" by itself. Instead we trained them to apologize and ask for forgiveness. This doesn't just protect relationships from offense building up, but it also begins to train children how to own their mistakes and to humble themselves.

It is also a regular practice in our house for us to apologize to our kids. Let's face it, in parenting, we mess up. We get frustrated, get short with them, or respond contrary to who we want to be. When this happens, my husband and I humble ourselves and ask forgiveness from our children. Just because we are the parent it doesn't give us the right to treat children with disrespect. Humbling yourself to your children will keep the lines of communication open. It will show them that you also make mistakes, and it establishes the precedence for the family.

> Let's face it, in parenting, we mess up. Forgiveness opens the lines of communication.

Another place where we align our actions with our values is that we have decided will be a full, free and fun family. I have looked for other words to describe this because the alliteration bothers me, but it has stuck with us. Because this is a value for our family, we teach about the responsibility we each have to get rid of the things that keep us from being free. We want to be the fullest family you meet. We want to fully embrace ourselves and we want to fully embrace each other. But holding this value means that when we act out of alignment with our character or our identity, we call each other on it.

Living Your Family's Values

One day, Kai was being a stinker of a boy and picking on his older sister. She was getting really frustrated with him and came to me with her complaint about it. I asked her if that was who Kai really was, and she said, "No. He loves me."

She knew who Kai was to her, even though he wasn't acting in accordance to it right then. We went in the other room together and by my leading, we reminded Kai who he was—a loving and caring brother. We spoke identity to him and over him. Then I asked Kai who he wanted to be. Did he want to be the pesky brother that caused his sister to doubt how he felt about her, or did he want to communicate clearly to his sister about how he loved her.

See, it's about choice. We are creating the opportunities for our children to align with who they really are. It's about creating a safe place for them to practice choosing who they are going to be. Kids are typically reactive. They react to their desires, to their opinions, and they react to their surroundings. But if we can create a space for them to step back and see that they are in the midst of a choice, we can help them to succeed.

One of our core values is that we mean what we say. Our yes means yes, and our no means no. There are many good books on parenting boundaries, and I would encourage you to read them. For the sake of this book, I am going to point out the importance of holding firm to the boundaries that you set. Following through with consequences shows your kids that you are trustworthy. Remember, we are developing our relationships as they grow. Boundaries create safety for kids to thrive and flourish, and it is important that they are able to trust the boundary setter. If you want to read more on this, I recommend Danny Silk's book, *Loving our Kids on Purpose*, and also *Parenting with Love and Logic* by Foster Cline and Jim Fay. Both of my books are worn and tattered from use. For those with young ones, *Love and Logic Magic for Early Childhood: Practical Parenting From Birth to Six Years* is particularly helpful .

These values are just a few we focus on. There are more that I haven't elaborated on. But the point is that whatever you do, do it with intentionality and do it with vision. If we are going to teach alignment and choosing to our kids, we need to know what we are aligning them with.

Tools to Bring Alignment

In my quiet time I once saw a picture that clarified alignment for me. I saw a vertical magnet. I saw a person to the left of the magnet. A word was spoken that pulled him back to center, like a magnet would. It was the vigorous kind of pull that the attraction of two magnets create. Jesus spoke to me that this is what a word in season will do. It will pull a person back to center when the word connects with their heart. This is what alignment is about. As a parent, when you see your child off-center, you can encourage and speak life over them, causing them to be magnetically drawn back to the center. It is important to remember that you as the parent are not defined by the choices of your children. It is your job to parent well, but they have the responsibility to choose.

Sometimes, they choose wrong, and it is not a reflection of who you are. It is a choice that they made. Don't confuse the two. Take the weight of their decision off of your shoulders.

There are several tools that we use as a family to help us align ourselves with who we want to be. One of those tools is simply making sure that our words reflect who we are and what we want to accomplish. The Bible says that life and death are in the power of the tongue. We purpose to keep our tongue speaking life. We have been given the image of a creator God. We create our world with our words. If our attitude or our words are not reflecting truth, we gently nudge ourselves and our children to align with what we want. One of the phrases that my kids hear me say all the time is, "I don't want to know what you don't want, I want to know what you do want." We don't want to complain and gripe, we want to co-labor with God to create our world. We often have to work through the issues of their heart to see what it is that they are truly after.

We make sure our words reflect who we are and what we want to accomplish.

One of the advantages of having our children speak about what they do want is the opportunities created for us to pray together about what is really important to them. We get to partner together towards what matters to them, even if it is only as simple as getting a snow cone or finding a lost toy. We have created a place for them to practice hearing the voice of God, we have partnered with them, and we have created a testimony. This is much better than getting flustered with them about their frustration and their gripes.

One day Kai was throwing a fit, griping because we had to go run errands. Mind you, he was only three at the time. He was telling me all that he was grumpy about so I asked him, "Kai tell me why you are so upset. What is it that you want to do?"

He calmed down and identified that he thought he was going to get to play with a friend that day. Little did he know that after the errands were finished we were going to, in fact, go play with that friend. After a simple explanation, we moved past the issue. Had I just reacted to the tantrum, I would have missed the opportunity to confirm that what he wanted was as important to me as what I wanted. It built trust.

Simple Truth

Kids are smarter than we give them credit for, but they are also simpler than we realize. Jesus has often had me simplify His truths to a single phrase or plain expression to help them receive and understand. To be honest, they help me receive truth too! They are typically prophetic acts that help us keep aligned.

One of the things we do in our family is that we rub in the truth. When people receive compliments, kind words or encouragement they get a little nervous and uncomfortable and don't know how to let them sink in. So when someone in our family gets a sweet word, we take our hand and rub it into our heart. I encourage the kids to rub it in deep so they don't let it get away. There is something powerful to purposefully receiving kind words and this little exercise helps them to do just that.

Another prophetic act I do with my kids is to ask for their eyes. When kids feel shame, regret, or are just not connecting with you, they typically look down. So, I ask for their eyes. What I am doing is intentionally getting their eyes connected with my eyes. There is scientific proof that you recognize within just moments of being with someone if you are accepted. When you purposefully get their eyes, you are speaking through the shame and letting them know that even when they mess up, you will connect with them. That you will receive them. That you love them.

You often hear the modeling industry refer to smiling with your eyes. This means to show emotion to someone through the expression in just your eyes. Well, when you get your kid's eyes, it is important that you give them purposeful emotion through your eyes. You want them to feel received, loved, and safe. Soften your gaze and purposely show kindness to them through your expression. It may sound silly, but it works. Remember that the eyes are the window to the soul, so show them how you heart and soul feel about them.

Facing Fear

One of the things young children can struggle with is fear. I remember when I first realized that my oldest, Adie, was beginning to experience this emotion. When she was young, her favorite movie was Finding Nemo. We had probably watched it at least a couple dozen times, but this one morning it was different. When the shark scene came on, she started panicking. She was afraid. She had begun processing fear. I remember feeling a check in my spirit, and the Lord asking me to go and give her a tool to deal with it. I sat down next to her, got her eyes, and said the simple phrase, "No fear, Adie. No fear."

She looked at me, and saw that I was okay. I asked her to repeat after me, to tell that fear that it couldn't stay. She followed my lead, and assertively said, "No fear."

I then heard the Lord ask me to sit with her while she faced her fear . See, even when we face fear, it is a matter of choosing to look it head on and not give it ground in our soul. When we are facing fear, Jesus comes and sits with us and gives us the strength to face it, because we are not alone. It is His perfect love that casts out all fear.

This phrase has become a staple in our home. We all will speak out when we start feeling afraid, "No fear!" As a family we have chosen to look at our fears, knowing that we are not alone in doing so. We are supported by each other, and we are supported by Him. If fear takes root in our hearts, it will begin to whittle away at our dreams, at our confidence, and at our security. Giving your children tools to help them deal with fear at a young age will give them the tools to fight the fears that want to rob them of true life.

In parenting choice in young children, much of what you are doing is teaching them to deal with their emotions. Emotions are strong and are indicators of a healthy individual. It is only as we get older that we begin to stuff emotions, or even worse, to turn off our hearts so that we stop feeling all together. Emotions are good, healthy, and necessary parts of life. Love and compassion are not just actions, they are actions and choices filled with emotion that will break the bond of the enemy. To feel deeply is to be free. But emotions need to be trained. They can rule you if you don't submit them to truth. That is what you, as a parent, are teaching your child. You are teaching them to deal with the frustration, the fear, the anger and the disappointment. When you have a basic understanding about how to handle emotions, you have the ability to keep your heart open. And isn't that what we all want … a heart that is open and a heart that feels deeply?

One day, my Zoe was struggling having the ability to face a fear. She needed to go and get her Minnie Mouse doll out of her room. The hall light was on, but it was dark in her room. I could have gone in and turned on her light, but I look for safe opportunities to practice facing our fears. I would rather her have a history and memory of overcoming fear that she can use when I am not around, than shield her from the opportunity to feel the feeling at all. I am not advocating that if your child is struggling with terror, that you create opportunities to face it. Use common sense, and more than anything be sensitive to the leading of the Holy Spirit.

Since this was a safe situation it provided a teachable moment. So I looked at her and said, "Zoe, I have lots of brave. Do you want some of mine?"

"Sure, Mommy!" she answered.

I reached my hand to my heart and grabbed some imaginary "brave," and handed it to her. I instructed her to put it in her heart. She gently placed her hand over her heart, smiled, then ran off to get her stuffed animal. When she came back, I celebrated with her. "You did it! You were brave! You faced that fear and did it!"

An act this small can instill courage in your child to believe that they can face their fear. It is simple, but it is effective.

Kids love practical expressions that help them learn how to deal with their hearts. Parenting intangible ideas with kids is easier if you give them something tangible to do. Abstract ideas need practical expression for young children to begin to grasp them. Practical expression creates movement where teaching can't.

Good-bye Grumpy

When my kids are grumpy we talk about how "happy" is their choice. Sometimes there is a reason they are not happy, and if so, we try to deal with it. But many times, they are just grumpy. A little thing set them off, and they don't know how to get back to a happy state. Many parents try to distract children out of the "grumpy," but what if instead of deploying distraction, the opportunity was leveraged allowing the child to practice choosing? Choosing is where they gain a history of victory—victory they chose.

I like to get animated with my kids, so when they are grumpy we pull all of our "grumpy" out of our hearts. Sometimes it is simple, and sometimes we pull and pull ... and pull ... like the clown taking out his handkerchiefs. We playfully remove all of the grumpy, and then I ask them to get rid of it. Sometimes we will literally go throw the grumpy in the trash. If we are in the car, we will throw it out of the window. And then sometimes, we picture handing the grumpy to Jesus.

Which way you handle it is up to you, to the moment, and to the Holy Spirit. The important thing is to teach our children that they have authority over their state of being. They get to choose what their life looks like. They, and we, are not succumbed to the ebbs and flows of life. We are made to live as Jesus intended, with the fruits of the Spirit manifesting in our life. But, we must partner with the Holy Spirit to see the joy. We must partner with the Holy Spirit to see the peace. He gives it, but we must choose to receive it. And to receive it, we have to be okay with letting go of a lesser reality. We let go of our grumpy to embrace His happy.

When I feel the atmosphere of my kids starting to change for the negative, I'll say, "Happy face freeze!" They put on their smiles or silly faces, and we keep them there until our moods begin to change. Does putting a smile on remove frustration? Not always, but you should try it. It is almost impossible to stay frustrated if you are smiling. Now, when Momma is in a bad mood, the kids will shout, "Happy face freeze!" And I will sit there and smile until my atmosphere shifts back to one that aligns with heaven. Even if the root of my frustration isn't dealt with, I now have the ability to handle it with a level head.

Lying, Leave

My Kai boy had a tendency to tell little lies. We had parented him through it, gone after it with truth, but it was difficult for him to stop protecting himself by telling lies. He even began to lie about little insignificant matters; things that wouldn't even get him in trouble. After much frustration and some prayer, I felt like his issue was recognizing that choice—the choice to tell lies or to tell truth.

When we started addressing the lies that were on his tongue and teaching him about his choice to give lies or to give truth, it began to change. Normally, I would want to understand his motives, go after why he was lying … what he was covering up, and why did he feel he needed to do this, etc.? But that approach wasn't working. What began to help him align his words and his heart with truth was recognizing the choice.

When he would lie, I would ask him if he had those lies on his tongue. He began to recognize them, and then we started adding practical acts to help him process the choice. He takes the lies off of his tongue in whatever creative way he has that day, and then we get rid of them. Practical simple things add tangible weight to the truths that you are instilling into your sweet little ones.

Powerful Play

I am uber-convicted to remain playful with my kids. John 10:10 is one of my favorite passages. Jesus tells us that the thief comes to kill, steal, and destroy, but He has come to give life and life abundantly. Abundant life is full. It is free. It is fun. It promotes living and thriving … not just surviving. It is full of laughter and grace. It is full of surprise and innocence. It is full. Children are full of life when they are playing. If you make aligning to Jesus rigid and cold, it will be hard to keep them engaged. They love playing. Make truth fun and play with your kids. There are many times when we identify that we need a particular fruit of the Spirit. One of us will use our imagination and go pick it off of Jesus' tree, and then come and give it to the person who is struggling. We then put the fruit in their heart and speak that word over them until their atmosphere begins to change. This is not just a simple exercise. You carry the authority of heaven! You can release that atmosphere upon others. This is what we do when we are

> **You carry the authority of heaven! You can release that atmosphere upon others.**

practicing the laying on of hands, we are releasing His atmosphere through our touch. We are carriers of Him and of His glory realm. Release it, especially upon your children.

I am a firm believer that we parent choice differently when our kids know Jesus and when they don't. We never want to dismiss the need for Jesus. When our kids made mistakes before they were saved, part of the way we parented that choice was to reveal the character and the need for Jesus. It was about revealing His grace and His love to them despite their choices. Remember the goal is for our kids to know Jesus, to walk with Him and embrace their truest identity.

When my children received Jesus, our parenting style changed some. Though we still focus on who He is, what He offers us, and our choices, we now have this wonderful ally called the Holy Spirit living inside of them. Paul and I began to hear Jesus teach us how to partner with Him and His leading. Remember, it is the Holy Spirit who convicts and leads us into all truth (John 16:13). Don't get me wrong, partnering with the Holy Spirit in parenting is not all about behavior, but we are talking about alignment and choosing truth. Because our children now have the Holy Spirit living in them, when a bad choice is made, we will sit back and allow Him to speak to their little hearts—we actually make space for it, waiting instead of immediately adjusting. To dismiss the voice of the Lord to them even though they are small would be foolish.

You may have heard it said that children do not have a "junior" Holy Spirit. It's true. The very Spirit that raised Christ from the dead lives within their little bodies and He is as powerful in them as He is within you! Just like in the example with Zoe having an opportunity to face her fear, we have chosen to leave room for our children to hear the voice of the Holy Spirit themselves. You can't formulate it or make it a system, because it is a cooperation that you have with Him. It is always sweet to my heart when my kids hear Holy Spirit talking to them about their choices. Choose consciously to work with Him. No matter where your child is standing, parenting choice and teaching alignment can be practical, fun, and fruitful.

CHAPTER FIVE

SIMPLE SAYINGS

Children crave consistency. They love it. They thrive when it exists. Consistency breeds confidence and trust in their hearts. When children know their boundaries, they know your expectations. One of my favorite parenting tools is what I call simple sayings. Simple sayings are words or phrases used often to reiterate a specific point. By using them frequently, their meaning is repeated in context until it is easily recognized and understood by your kids. You are reinforcing breakthroughs in the behaviors and attitudes of your children every time they are used. The purpose of simple sayings is to convey your message in a simplistic, consistent way.

I use simple sayings all the time. You probably do too and didn't even know it. There are phrases you say again and again, without even thinking. These are your simple sayings. When you make them an intentional parenting tool, they are effective in helping you raise your kids.

I have already used several of my simple sayings in this book. They are scattered throughout my chapters. Because they have been so useful in helping me set expectations with my children, and have made life with three much less frustrating, I want to draw specific attention to my favorite simple sayings.

"I love you all the time with all my heart."

I noticed that when I was frustrated with them, my kids wanted the security of knowing how I felt about them. At first I would say, "I love you when I'm mad. I love you when I'm sad. I love you when I'm happy, and I love you when I'm glad. I love you all the time with all my heart." Eventually this saying got shortened to just the last phrase, "I love you all the time with all my heart." It is simple, memorable, and underlines my "all" commitment of love to my kids.

"You are part of this family and that will never change."

This saying came as a direct counter to a lie my daughter was believing. After the lie left, the simple saying remained. I love the structure of family and want to reinforce the foundations as often as I can. I remind my children on a regular basis that they belong, not just to a family … but to a family as awesome as ours!

"I love you me."

When Zoe was a baby, I would tell her, "I love you," and she would reply, "I love you me." It became our personal saying of affection. It is a simple saying that is personal to us—to Zoe and me. I have simple sayings that are specific to each of my children. They each treasure them, and love the uniqueness given to them.

Regardless of how you speak your love, speak it. Never let a day pass without conveying the emotions and love that you feel for you children. A lack of communication about love can lead to scars on the heart that affect even the most adapted adults. Be diligent and be creative. Say "I love you," but don't stop there. Allow yourself to speak love with other simple sayings.

"Give me your hands and eyes."

When there is something I want my children's attention for I will say, "Give me your hands and eyes." When they hear me say this, my kids know they need to hold my hands and look me in the face. For most children, when you really want their attention, you need to touch them. Physical touch keeps them from being as distracted when you want to speak to them. I can tell if they are listening when I make eye contact with them. I use this saying to speak different kinds of things. I will use it in discipline, but I also use it to affirm. I don't want the only times that I look purposely into their eyes to be when they are in trouble.

If you are speaking to them for the sake of discipline, make sure you have kind eyes (not angry or hard eyes). The point of looking in their eyes is so they see that you still have love towards them. Your eyes are the window to your soul, and you convey acceptance to them from your eyes. Be deliberate about conveying acceptance to them, even in discipline. It shows them that you are safe, even in their mistakes. There are also times when I want to affirm that I am proud of them and I will say, "Give me your eyes." This causes us all to slow down and embrace the moment. When you connect with your eyes, you are inviting connection with your heart. I purpose to connect my eyes with my children's eyes every day.

"Rub it in."

When I want my children to be intentional about receiving a compliment or a word of encouragement, they will often hear, "Rub it in." We will physically take our hand and "rub" the compliment in. I want them to work truth into their hearts. I want it to sink in. Reminding ourselves that we need to receive causes our walls to go down and for us to let the affirmation in.

"Have you talked to them about it?"

I am very blessed to have children that love each other. Many times the reason my Kai gets in trouble is not because he is wrestling with the girls, but because he is giving them affection too viciously! When problems do arise between them, there are several simple sayings I inevitably come back to. One that rolls off of my lips almost every day is, "Have you talked to them about it?" Tattling and bickering is going to happen. We desire to instruct them to handle problems and conflicts like they are handled in scripture. In Matthew 18 we are instructed that if we have an issue with our brother, we need first to go to him. This is how we parent conflict. I want my children to learn to work out their issues amongst themselves. I will tell them to, "Give them your heart." What this really means is, "You need to go tell you brother how this made you feel. You need to handle it, not me."

"Is your heart happy ... ?"

I desire long-term connection with my family, all of us. I want my children to learn how to communicate without me being in the middle of it. If they are unable to deal with the matter themselves, then both of them come and talk to me or my husband about it. But they have to have first tried themselves. Once we have dealt with it, I will ask, "Is your heart happy with them?" This simple saying comes out of my mouth regularly. When you value connection, it is important to uphold the connection you have.

After my kids and I are moving past discipline I will ask them, "Is your heart happy with mom?" I want them to answer honestly. It doesn't mean that I will fix how they feel, but if there is something I can offer, then I want to offer it. Also, if my heart is not happy with them, then I will use this phrase to let them know. More than one time, it has kept my tongue from saying something filled with bitterness out of frustration. Having a simple saying has helped me guard my tongue.

"Words are power."

Often when kids are frustrated, they will resort to acting out. Some kids scream, bite, or hit to make their point known. I try to encourage a healthy way to deal with their internal frustration by using the simple saying, "Words are power." My kids were repeating this simple phrase almost as soon as they could talk.

Teaching even toddlers that words are power, not yelling, is important. As they have gotten older, we talk about how words create realities. If we don't like what is happening, we can use our words to create a new reality. This encourages them to talk to one another, and to even address the atmosphere that is around them. "Words are power" also reminds them that there is a responsibility to use kind words. Mean words hold the power to hurt, honest words hold the power to connect, and kind words hold the power to encourage and heal.

"Obey all the way, the first time."

We expect obedience in our household. Disobedience is a symptom. It reveals an underlying problem. We will be intentional about getting to the root, but obedience is still a value. "Obey all the way, the first time" is the simple saying I use. It conveys what I want in the relationship, and it gives them an expectation.

"Ahhh, man. That's so sad."

When my children are not listening and obeying, I use a simple saying for that as well. "Ahhh, man. That's so sad." I learned from Love and Logic that this phrase can alert them to when they have crossed the line without you having to yell. It has worked for me to have a saying that I go back to over and over again. They know when they hear it, they have disobeyed. Anything that helps me alleviate confusion and frustration is of benefit to me and to them.

"You guys will always be good friends."

A friend of mine was telling me how her mom always encouraged her and her siblings that they would always be good friends. And, truthfully, they are some of the closest siblings I know. I have adopted their saying as one of my simple sayings. I frequently remind my kids by saying, "You guys will always be good friends." It is a prophetic declaration of connection and unity.

"Family first, no matter the cost."

We desire for our children to understand that regardless of all of the pulls of the rest of the world, our family is our priority. "Family first, no matter the cost" is our simple saying. They always have our first attention. We will be faithful in our family before we will be faithful with the world.

"Asked and answered."

My children will often ask the same question, hoping for a different answer. They ask it repetitively, somewhat like a battering ram, trying to knock down the wall. My simple saying keeps my frustration down. I heard it from someone else and quickly adopted it. For each subsequent question, my response is, "Asked and answered." It is simple. It makes them think and recall my answer, and it keeps me peaceful.

"Go get your squeals out."

I have a squealy kid. It doesn't seem to matter where Zoe is, she will yell. She has something to say, and she wants somebody to listen. Paul's great-grandmother had a porch that she would send the kids out to deal with their issues. I adopted the idea, and we have a squealing porch. They hear, "Inside voice," all the time. If they can't take their tone down, I will follow it with, "Go get your squeals out." They will go stand on the front porch and squeal as loud and as long as they want. When they come back in, I'll ask them if the squeals are all out, and if so they get to come back in. If not, they go squeal some more. Our neighbors may wonder what I am feeding them, but the volume in the house remains manageable.

"I don't receive that."

When words are spoken about us that are lies, we are intentional about not taking them into our heart as our own. "I don't receive that," is a staple in our house. We choose truth. We don't let the enemy or our fears set our reality. We let the word of God and what He says about us be what we stand on.

"Happy face freeze!"

In realizing that we have the power to choose our reality, I will use the phrase, "Happy face freeze!" We do this silly and we do it fun, but it works. It is impossible to give a real smile and stay grumpy. We want to choose joy. It is what Christ came to give us, a life that is full and fun. This simple saying can get us over the bumps. I will also remind them that they have the power to change their attitude by saying, "Change your heart." Whatever comes out is a reflection of what they are feeling and what is getting in. To change an attitude, we may need to adjust what is going in. Trying to adjust a behavior without addressing the root and the heart will be futile. Take the time to work to the bottom of their feelings. Help them change their heart.

"You choose or I choose."

When giving my children choices, they will hear, "You choose, or I choose." I use this phrase to give them a place to make a choice, but the choice is not open-ended. They have a responsibility to choose, or I will make the choice for them.

"Do you need some brave?"

We love taking the overflow from our life and giving it to each other. "Do you need some brave?" is the practical way we do this. I will take some brave out of my heart and hand it to them. Kids love tangible ways to receive, and this one is one of my favorites. We have the ability to encourage, literally to "put in courage." I am intentional about offering their spirits and their hearts what they need. It may change from brave to joy or even to love as we fill each other up with what we are lacking. One of my favorite things to do with Adie is when we give each other love. She loves it. We both put our hands on each other and we push all of the love we feel for each other into the other person. We get silly, but we focus on tangibly releasing our feeling. It literally will change both of our attitudes. Giving love will shift your atmosphere, you have been forewarned!

"Because you are a McClendon."

Recently we have added a new simple saying. It started when Kai had thrown trash down on the ground. I asked him to pick it up, and he responded with,"Why?"

I spouted off, "Because McClendon's don't do that, we take care of things."

It answered his questions, but it gave me a new simple saying. I now will often respond with, "Because you are a McClendon," followed by whatever needs to be attached. There are certain values that we as a family hold, and I apply this saying when we are bumping against one of those values. Regardless of your families values and sayings, be intentional about reinforcing their breakthroughs with simple sayings.

Simple sayings are an easily adaptable tool to add to your belt. You can adopt some of mine or create your own, but they will help keep you consistent as a parent. When you are consistent, you give your children the expectations they need to be able to succeed.

CHAPTER SIX

GATHER STONES

I will never forget the day I found a large box of rocks under our bed. My husband Paul and I were not even one year into marriage, and while spring cleaning I found an old box of his. When I get motivated to purge the house, everything is game. I looked at Paul with great hope that this box could be discarded. His offense at my question startled me. He said, "These are *my* rocks."

Apparently my facial expression didn't communicate that I understood, so he picked up one stone and told me where he was when he found it, what was going on, and why it was important. After a fifteen minute crash course on "his rocks," I agreed they were worth keeping. Each rock spoke to Paul. He had gathered stones from all over the world, and they were part of his story.

As parents, we are called to gather "stones" for our children. We are called to collect the stones—memories and memorials—that have meant something to them. We are called to oversee and treasure their collection until they can do so for themselves. The stones I am referring to are not the physical rocks, of course, but the moments of encounter our children experience with Jesus.

Faith Markers

We have always raised our children with an expectation of the supernatural. We pray for each other's healing, and we press in (work in faith towards) to raise the dead. For a long time, the only practice we had on raising the dead was with the plants mommy had somehow let die! But one day while playing outside, Adaiah ran up to me with this frantic look on her face. "There's a dead gecko on the front step!" she exclaimed, her eyes wide with a look of disgust on her face.

My son typically rescues my daughters from the bugs. Let's just say, my daughters have embraced their girly side. But on this particular day, Adaiah was genuinely disturbed by the dramatic demise of the gecko. We had just prayed for a plant that was struggling, speaking life over it, so this was fresh in Adie's mind. I asked her what we should do about the little gecko. She looked me in the eyes with determination and calmly replied, "We should pray for it."

That is just what she did. She crouched down over this squished, smashed gecko and said, "Be raised in Jesus' name."

Nothing happened.

She looked up at me, a little unsure and asked, "Should I do it again?"

"Yes, I think you should," I answered.

Adie leaned over the gecko and spoke, "Life, in Jesus' name."

Then she said one more time with unction, "Life!" and commanded the gecko to rise.

All of a sudden, that little lifeless gecko began to get his color back and in a moment he wiggled, then scampered off!

Skeptical? Wondering if this little guy was really dead? I have dealt with my share of little creatures—this guy was beyond gone. There was not even an ounce of life in him. Jesus commands us to preach the Gospel, to heal the sick, and raise the dead. This command is to all believers. This is our call. That day, on our porch, the faith of a child and the power of God were released on a lifeless gecko.

This is a stone. This is a treasure. This is a story of faith that needs to be remembered. When we are building our faith in who God is to us and through us, we need to remember how He shows up. It is important to not only treasure these moments for yourself, but to collect these stones for your children. There are markers in your walk with Jesus and in you discovering His identity that you can recall off the top of your head. When you are raising your children to encounter Jesus, don't forget to collect the stones of their stories. They are faith markers.

Remember

Many times in both the Old and New Testaments we are instructed to remember. Remember. Remember what He has done. Remember who He is. Gather stones. Remember.

In the Old Testament, Joshua led the Israelites over the Jordan River on dry ground (Joshua 4). The Lord instructed Joshua to have twelve men, one from each tribe, collect stones out of the middle of the Jordan River. They were then to carry these stones to where they were camping. They were set together as a remembrance of what God did for them that day. The scripture says the stones were to be a sign among them; that they were to be a memorial to the people of Israel forever that God is a living God who acts on behalf of His people.

God commanded Joshua to have them gather stones. These stones were to be a sign, a memorial to what the Lord had done that day. When Jesus shows up for your children, gather the stones, collect their stories. The stones that Joshua had the Israelites gather remained in Gilgal. They served not only as a reminder, but the stones also created a place where God could be continually honored. Gilgal was a place that could be revisited and returned to.

One day, I hired a babysitter, Staci, to get some errands completed. When I returned our sweet friend and trusted sitter told us how she had struggled with a headache all day long. She still had it, and we decided to pray for her. So my husband and I pressed in for the headache to leave. When we finished praying, not much had changed, but Kai came into the room and asked why we were praying. We explained about Staci's headache. He looked kinda perplexed, then went over to Staci, and reached up by her head. With hand motions, he pulled the headache out. Then he went and threw the headache in the trash. He told her, "Jesus doesn't want you to have a headache."

Staci looked at me, kinda shocked, and exclaimed, "My headache is gone! When Kai pulled it out … it was gone!"

This was a stone I could gather for Kai. I went to him later that night and asked him how he felt when he prayed for Staci. He said, "I knew it wasn't right. Jesus wanted her headache gone."

This moment of remembering captured the truth of what happened for Kai. I don't want to gather stones for them out of my memory, I want to capture the moment for him—with him. I want Kai to remember how he felt when faith came upon him. I want him to remember how he felt when Staci was so excited that Jesus showed up for her when he prayed. I want him to remember the moment, not just for the purpose of having a story. I want to gather the stone to teach him that when he submits to Jesus, he can be used to bless others. I want to gather the stone to remind him that Jesus will use him again for healing.

Capture the Moments

When we gather stones for our children, we are gathering the places where they have encountered God. We capture their emotions. We capture their wonder. We capture their joy. We are in essence collecting their testimony. One of the amazing things about testimonies is that they carry the power to do the same thing again. Testimonies are living and breathing acts of God. They are not sterile stories, they carry life and power to accomplish the same thing again.

When my husband came home from work with a headache, what did I do? I went and got Kai. I pulled out the stone that we had gathered. I reminded him of how he felt and what Jesus did through him. I reminded him that even at his age, Jesus could and would work through him. When Kai laid hands on his dad, he was full of courage that Jesus could take daddy's headache away just like He took Staci's headache away. Kai had a testimony here, and it had not been lost in the busy-ness of life. It had been collected and treasured.

Not every stone collected needs to be a big one. They don't all have to be about the supernatural. Remember to collect the pebbles and rocks of everyday life too. These places hold stories of God's faithfulness and character as well. One day, Zoe had carried her blanket into the store without me knowing it, and we left it behind. I didn't even realize it was missing until that evening, and since I was unaware she had taken it into the store, I scoured the house from top to bottom. I searched the car at least five times, but to no avail. This was *the* blanket, and we were in trouble.

Everyday life holds opportunities for God's faithfulness and character to become part of our story.

We looked for several days before I realized it could be at that store. I called them and described the blanket, and was informed that they had emptied their lost and found box that morning, but a blanket just like the one I was describing had been in the box. I felt sick to my stomach. It was the blanket—Zoe's favorite blanket. The one that made nap times so much easier. The one she had since birth. The one that came from a company no longer in business … just great …

I sat down with Zoe and told her that her blanket had been at the store, but now it was gone. She was so sad. Too miserable to even cry any more she sighed softly, "I want a new one. I miss it." My heart was breaking. I had already scoured the internet and couldn't find another one like it. So with not much faith in my heart, we asked Jesus to redeem the situation.

That same day, Paul had gone into a store and just happened to go by the baby section. Right there on the shelf was a pink blanket. It was made of the same material, and looked just like Zoe's lost blanket. All that was missing was a heart patch that had been on the previous one. Paul brought it to us that evening and Zoe was so excited! I was so relieved. I wasn't sure how she would handle the replacement. She knew it wasn't her blanket, but she said it was just as soft. She was genuinely blessed by it and I went over to collect the stone.

"Zoe," I said, "Do you remember us crying this morning about your blanket being gone?"

She nodded, "Yes."

"Do you remember us asking Jesus to make the situation better?" I asked.

She nodded again, "Yes."

I smiled and hugged her, "Jesus heard us. He saw you, Zoe. Jesus cares about what is important to you."

I gathered the stone for her. This stone was something Jesus did solely to bless Zoe. Paul had stumbled upon it, and I hadn't had faith. It was a stone that revealed His heart for her.

Now every time Zoe misplaces her blanket (unfortunately, it happens frequently) we ask Jesus where it is and ask Him to bring it back to her … and it happens! We find it shortly after and I remind Zoe that Jesus sees her, and that what is important to her is important to Him. We gathered the stone and we remember who He was to us that day.

Warring With Stones

Another reason we gather stones is to war with them. In 1 Samuel 17, David is set to fight Goliath. It was a battle that was not won with sword or spear, it was a battle won with stones. David collected five stones and faced the giant. He was physically outmatched with the Philistine, but he walked in with his testimony. He had killed the lion. He had killed the bear. He knew that God would deliver him from the enemy. He had testimony. He warred with stones.

There are battles and challenges our children will face that will feel large and overwhelming. We can remind ourselves of the testimony of Jesus to our children. We can remember He showed up for our kids. We have stones we have gathered that we can war with. We, just like David, can come out of the battle victorious because of the grace of our God.

Encounter Again

In our family, we frequently tell the stories that go with the stones we have gathered. We practice remembering, but we do it in a way that encourages us to meet with God again. Our stories are not to be just stories. They are to be invitations to encounter God again. In Matthew 4, Jesus was tested in the wilderness. The enemy came to Him, and taunted Him by encouraging Him to turn the stones into bread. Jesus responded by saying, "Man does not live by bread alone, but by every word that proceeds from the mouth of God."

Jesus instructed me to make sure that when we gather stones for our children and when we remember our encounters, that we do not make them our bread. Our stories do not feed our souls, they remind us of encounters with the Jesus that did. There is a difference. If we elevate the stone (the memory) over the encounter, we miss the point. We remember so we can encounter again. We remind ourselves of His character to us and through us so that we have a foundation of faith.

We remember so we can enounter again.

In Matthew 7:9-11, Jesus says, *"Which of you, if your son asks for bread, will give him a stone? Or if he asks for a fish, will give him a snake? If you, then, though you are evil, know how to give good gifts to your children, how much more will your Father in heaven give good gifts to those who ask Him!"*

We serve a good God. We wants us to be full! When we are hungry, He does not give us a stone, He gives us bread. When we need an encounter, He gives us a fresh one. We gather stones to remember, but we do this so that we remember to eat of His manna frequently. We feed ourselves on new experiences, and then we have new testimonies and new stones to add to our foundation of faith.

Ask for bread. Encounter His character and His faithfulness in your life and in the lives of your children. Gather stones and be encouraged to go and eat more bread. The stones are to remind us to encounter again. Enjoy the cycle of His goodness to you.

Remember. Encounter. Remember. Encounter.

CHAPTER SEVEN

I DON'T RECEIVE THAT

"If you know the enemy and know yourself, you need not fear the result of a hundred battles. If you know yourself but not the enemy, for every victory gained you will also suffer a defeat. If you know neither the enemy nor yourself, you will succumb in every battle."

— SUN TZU, *The Art of War*

Whether we like it or not, we are in a war. A war that has opposing forces. Good and evil. Godly and ungodly. We are smack dab in the middle of an epic battle. Although the end has been decided and Jesus has already won, we still have the privilege of allocating His victory in our hearts and in this world. But, we fight from a different reality. We fight from heaven. We don't have to strive for a victory, we can rest in Jesus and allocate what He already gave us.

Knowing who we are in Christ is essential. Walking in our God-given authority, living out our "I Ams," keeps us true to our nature. The enemy comes to us speaking lies about the nature of God, speaking lies about who we are, and who we aren't. We need to know how to discern the lies from the truth.

Making your family a safe place to talk about hard things is necessary to move forward in this, especially with young children. If you are not aware of their thoughts, how can you parent the truth in those places? Yes, the Lord will speak to us about their hearts, but we should foster open dialogue with them about hurt places and create a safe place to share inner thoughts. This sounds easy, but it's not. If your child is going to develop the trust necessary to let you into these places, you will need to lay down your need to be right and let go of your personal ego. Kids interpret life from their reality—through the filter of their emotions and knowledge. Many of their conclusions can get convoluted out of a lack of maturity. Their thoughts may offend you because they missed your heart entirely in their interpretation. To be able to parent these places, you will need to remain humble and open. It is silly to think that a two-year old's opinion can hurt your feelings, but we all know that when we pour love into places of their hearts and it isn't received, it can hurt.

If you notice that your child's feeling are hurt, start by asking them why. You might be surprised by their answers. As you begin to teach children how to put words to their emotions, they get good at it quickly. Ask with a desire to get to the root of their pain, don't just address the action that stems from it. If we parent the action only, we will continue to fight the same battle ... picking only one dandelion at a time while dozens spring up. Until we get to the root of the problem and address it with them, it is never really settled.

Loose Them From The Lie

One time with Adaiah, I totally botched a moment with her. I spewed my frustration out on her, and my words had cut her to the heart. I picked myself up from the mistake and apologized to her, but a few days later I recognized that her actions toward me had been reserved, somewhat timid. As I tucked her into bed, I asked her what was wrong.

Timidly, almost in a whisper she said, "I don't think … you want me … " she paused, " … to be part of the family." A huge sigh escaped her.

"Oh sweetie," I said, scooping her up in my arms, "why do you think that?" I hugged her tightly.

"When you … when you were mad at me," she sniffed, leaning against me like I might disappear, "I felt like … like you didn't want to be around me anymore." Her eyes were big and sad.

My heart melted.

The reason I had gotten mad at her earlier in the week had nothing to do with this thought. I was frustrated with her when her behavior towards her brother had been unkind, but my anger had made an impression on her. She had a sensitive place in her heart, and the enemy had spoken to it. He had begun to lie to her about her place in my life and in our family.

I quickly reassured her that it wasn't true, but also recognized that she had let that lie in. I asked the Lord for a strategy to uproot this simple lie that was causing her to lose her security in our family. We typically do our "I Am Statements" at night, and that night the Lord had me add a simple little phrase: "I am a part of this family, and that will never change. I am loved by my momma, loved by my daddy, loved by my Jesus, and I love myself."

I didn't want to address the lie just once. I wanted to remain intentional about the truth. It is the truth that sets you free (John 8:32). Speak the truth in love over your child, and watch the truth loose them from the lie. Had I hardened my heart or gotten offended at Adie for interpreting my frustration in that way, I would have missed what her heart was really feeling. When it is safe for children to share their emotions and feelings with you, they will. But if they get in trouble for what they feel, they will keep them bottled up inside, and you will miss moments like these that can bring freedom, connection, and can anchor them in truth. The affirmation of this phrase addressed the lie, and created a truth.

Foster an atmosphere of trust and safety with your children. When they are being vulnerable with their feelings and opinions, there are times that I have to bite my tongue to not correct them. Then there are times where it is easy to see them and easy to overlook the messy that is on the surface. Each moment will be different, but if you allow communication and connection to be a primary value, you will push past the awkward to parent the truth.

Replace Lies With Truth

Kai is made for justice. He fights for what he believes in and if someone puts a label on him that isn't true, he gets adamant about it. He will boldly declare, "That's NOT me!" ... and he means it! It hurts his feelings when he is misunderstood, but he rarely hides it. He fights back. Sometimes he fights back well, and sometimes he fights back with pushing and yelling. My job is not to teach him to stop fighting against the lie, but to teach him how to fight well. He is feisty for the truth, and that is God-given. "That's not me," is a great phrase, and it is enough to silence the lie. Kai is learning that his words matter and no further retaliation is necessary. If the lie lingers, we take the label that he didn't like, and we ask Jesus to speak about who Kai really is. His heart softens as soon as he hears the truth. Because his heart is already fighting the lie, Kai is usually hungry to replace it with truth.

The enemy won't just lie to them about who they are, but also about who they aren't. Both are detrimental. You aren't wanted. You are a disappointment. Both are lies. Both need to be dismantled.

The key is recognizing we have the ability to choose what we listen to and that we can teach our children how to discern the words they hear. Adaiah recently brought me a sheet of paper. It was a plea for truth. She had written, "Dear Mom, yesterday I thought that you did not like me. I thought that I didn't feel like a princess and I felt sad and cried because I did not feel with joy and I did not feel loved. Is it true?"

When she slipped it on the table and walked away, I felt mixed reactions. My heart was sad that she was hurting,

We have the ability to choose what we listen to and we can teach our children how to discern the words they hear.

but I also rejoiced that she recognized the feelings and instead of burying them and believing what her emotions felt, she was asking me if it was true. It is hard to read a note like that from your child, but I am so grateful that we have fostered an environment where the things she is feeling, she can safely bring to us. She is learning to think about the thoughts that she receives, not to just blindly accept them. This is victory because when we examine our thoughts, we can keep them in line with Jesus.

In 2 Corinthians we are admonished to take captive every thought and make them obedient to Christ. We are to be in charge of our "gates." Our gates are our eyes, ears, and mouth. We are responsible for what we let into our beings. We can let the lies in or we can keep them shut out. Just because we hear a lie, doesn't mean we have to receive it. We have personal responsibility for our thought life and our actions. Part of parenting identity is teaching our children how to recognize lies and giving them the tools they need to replace them with truth.

Remove Lies ... Forcibly if Necessary!

My Zoe loves being with her sister and brother. She loves playing with them and just being in the same room as them. Her feelings get hurt when she feels like they don't want to spend time with her. The enemy's voice will pervert what they have actually said to her, and she will drop her chin and her eyes, and sink away in sadness.

I'm not sure her dramatic nature is due to her personality or to the fact that she is the youngest, but she knows how to put flair on. When she believes a lie, we deal with it as dramatically as her personality is. When this happens, I go in and gently lift her head up. I remind her that she doesn't have to shrink in shame because the Lord is her shield (Psalm 3:3). We stand up together and we lift our chins up as high as we can. Then we talk about the lie surrounding her belonging. We remind ourselves of all of the things that show us that her siblings love her. Then we go over to the door and close it. We shut the door to the lie. We kick the lie out of our house. She will theatrically "kick" the lie out of the room and then often times, slam the door. Zoe understands choice best when she gets to display it as spectacularly as the rest of her life.

To be intentional about replacing it with truth, I will pull all three of them together and remind them how good it is when they live together in unity (Psalm 133). Then we take the time as a family to speak the truth to Zoe's heart. We each will speak something we love about her. I will have them hold hands and look each other in the eyes. I find that when we do this, all of our hearts let down their guards and we begin to let love in.

Children rise up to the expectations we set. I never want to set expectations so high that my children are working to perform for me, but I also don't want to set expectations that are laced with fear and the culture and way of the world. The world says that families are dysfunctional. The world says that as kids grow up, brothers and sisters argue and fight, and that connections gets lost. Fortunately, I don't live by the standard of the world, but by the grace of Jesus. I don't expect every day to be easy with my family, but I know we will remain connected. We are intentional towards it, and we receive grace from heaven to maintain it. We frequently set the expectation that love and connection are the norm in our family. We speak about how we choose to love each other and choose unity. We take time to minister to the places in each other's hearts that aren't feeling connected, just like we did with Zoe, because I believe that family can be functional. Not perfect, but functional. Functional family doesn't mean that dysfunction doesn't exist. It means that the family dynamic is centered around truth, health, and what Jesus is doing. It is not centered around sabotage, avoidance, and what the enemy is doing.

I Don't Receive That

I was washing the dishes one evening and had been struggling all day with thoughts about my inadequacy. There was a war raging inside of me because the lies felt so true, but my heart and my spirit knew they weren't. I was scrubbing away some grease stuck to a pan, and I just blurted out, "I don't receive that." My husband looked at me kinda strange, and I quickly assured him that it had nothing to do with him. As soon as I adamantly addressed the lies, peace fell over me. Addressing the lies is a basic warfare principle, but I had previously made it much more complex. This simple statement wrapped up all of the principles I had known, but took all of the unnecessary steps out of it. My family has adopted this phrase. When we hear a lie, or even just something that doesn't align with who we are, we will declare, "I don't receive that in Jesus' name."

This statement is simple enough for children, but more than powerful enough for adults. It is the conversation ender with the enemy. It shuts the lies down and brings you back to the place where you can ask about the truth. You have been made powerful and you have the ability to choose to dismiss the lies and to approach heaven about the truth. Be bold, be courageous, and ask Jesus the truth. Remember you can approach the throne of grace with confidence. Remember that the only real anchor of truth comes from the mouth of the One who is faithful and true. Dispel the lie, but don't stop there. Go to Jesus and secure your identity with His words. Do it for yourself and do it for your children. Make it a practice in your house and your children will grow up knowing the voice of Truth.

Dispel the lie and secure your identity with His words.

CHAPTER EIGHT

PARTNER WITH WHAT YOU FIND

My desire is to help fashion each of my children into the person God saw when He created them. I desire to mold and shape them by my words, actions, and prayers. In fact, one of my greatest convictions in parenting is to partner with what I find—to allow what is already in my children the freedom to emerge.

I desire to help them embrace their "I Am" statements and walk in freedom. Their identity covers them just as shoes cover their feet. Just as each child prefers different kinds of shoes—fashion boots, "running fast" shoes, or glittery heels, each child's identity covers them in a specific way, exactly suited for the path they are created to travel. If the shoe fits, wear it. If the identity fits, wear it.

No Two Alike

Each time I had another child, I wondered in what ways they would be like their siblings. Even though there are places of overlap, I was and still am amazed at how different each of them are. No two children are ever just alike, not even identical twins. The uniqueness of children is astounding.

I love learning about the way they think, the way they respond, and the way they operate. It gives me insight into how to connect with them. Their personalities, their gifts, and their talents are all different, and all reveal different things about the God they were made like. Proverbs 22 states, *"Train up a child in the way he should go, and when he is old he will not depart from it."* This verse has stuck with me for the entirety of my parenting. This is the verse often spoken about in regards to parenting. Many talk about it in reference to how we raise our kids to know Jesus and to know the truth. All of those teachings are good, but when conviction fell on me, this familiar verse took on a different meaning. The Lord spoke to me about knowing what made each of my kids tick, and raising them with the training they personally needed to walk in their identity, and ultimately their purpose.

The promise of this scripture is that if you raise each child with what they individually need, they will not depart from their path. The warning is that if you don't tap into the strategy for rearing each child, they are in danger of not knowing their way. If we look at many of the adults around us, they are still searching for their way. They are searching for their path. I desire to help my children know their path and have clear direction on which way they are to go. Be intentional about helping form that and helping them discover it.

Because each child is different, you must be willing to change or adapt your methods when parenting. Speak in pictures to those who need pictures and speak plainly to the child who needs simple truth. Don't expect your introvert to behave the same in public as your extrovert does. Work with Jesus to teach your child in the way that they will learn. Parenting is not a one-size-fits-all kind of venture. Find what speaks love to your child, and do it. Find what causes your kids to feel most connected, and then connect. Adjust, change, and partner with heaven to train each child in the way they should go.

It's Their Life—Not Yours

As you hear from Jesus about what is in each child, the picture of who they are begins to become clearer. As you watch them develop and engage life, passions start rising to the surface. Talents start emerging. When this happens, one of the things we have to do as parents is to keep our hopes, dreams, and expectations for their life in check. We need to make sure that we don't limit them to what we think they should do or become. We must remain open to a bigger picture we cannot even see yet.

We all have dreams for our children. Some of them are general, and some of them are more specific. What happens when our child interprets what is in their heart differently than we have? Will we trust them to follow their heart? Will we try to control them back to our expectation? These questions may seem premature for a book about young children, but they aren't. Answering these questions now will give you parameters for later. Deciding not to determine your children's future will guard your connection. It is your job to help them discover themselves, not to control the way their identity is poured out.

Making these decisions now will keep your heart in check when you find a treasure about your child. It is your job to steward that treasure and to help protect the map that guides them to discovering more. It is not your job to dictate to them what to do with that treasure.

When a child demonstrates an interest in something we may not value highly (or understand), it is easy to condition them away from their natural passion and towards a response we desire. Our feedback is their instructor. We

Our feedback is our children's instructor.

can unwittingly submerge the very gifts and natural abilities God equipped them with because it is completely different than how we were wired. Determining to guide your children rather than control them now when they are small will give you a plumb line on how to steward what you find. They will learn to trust your voice and in the future will seek your advice when they begin to navigate the world on their own.

In a practical sense, each child has a different mark of greatness. Adaiah is very driven and creative. She loves to sit down and create with words, drawings, and crafts. For me to expect the same kind of creativity from my other children would be requiring something from them that isn't in their nature. Zoe is a highly creative child as well, but her creativity is different than the kind I have seen in Adaiah.

Kai loves money. He loves doing chores to earn money, and oddly, he just has a way to find money. This is something distinct to him. For me to interpret how this will play out in his life could set him up to perform for approval versus stepping into his true purpose. What if because I see his knack for money, I begin to talk to him about being a banker? I could proclaim it over him and set my expectations that way. I could reward any play that surrounded banking and redirect other kinds of "make believe" that had to do with money.

But what if in his heart Kai really desired to be an entrepreneur that starts his own business and builds wealth. What if I demonstrate a bent towards having a "stable job with benefits" or commonly express an aversion to risk? The expectations from me and my interpretation of Kai's interests could do one of two things. First, it could keep him from pressing into what he wanted altogether. Or, if he did, it could create a rift in our relationship. Neither is a desirable outcome, and both can be avoided.

I can leave the discovery of his purpose to him. I am responsible to parent his identity into him, and train him in what we find. I can teach Kai money principles and principles of economics and help him discover what he enjoys as he grows. But ultimately the place he chooses to take it is his responsibility, not mine. I know that we have all seen relationships that have fallen apart because the parent expects the child to take over the family business, go to law school, or to become a doctor. Purpose to partner with their dreams, not to define them.

Honor

One of the greatest things that we can do for our children is to honor the gift of God that is in them. We treat with great regard and great respect the design of God in our kids. We choose not to trample what He said was good, and we bring to each child's attention the value of the way that Jesus created them.

Honor was a command to children from God. It is part of the Ten Commandments and with it, a promise of long life. Children learn how to honor from their parents. For children to honor us well, we honor them well. When we treat who they are with great honor, they learn what honor is. When we sow honor, we reap honor. We teach them that we honor others not because they deserve it, but because being honorable is who we are. We set an honorable tone in our relationships, and we abide by it.

We honor our children by listening to them. We honor our children by valuing their opinions, and we honor them by giving them respect. We choose to listen to their ideas, and to give them weight. If we really believe our children have something to offer, then we need to make sure that they have a safe place to offer themselves at home.

This can be simple. When Kai comes up with an idea for family night, we choose to listen and don't dismiss his idea because it wasn't something we came up with. When Zoe chooses to tell us the way that she sees the world, we give her view a safe place, recognizing that maturity will come. Create spaces where you can give your children permission to explore their purpose and ideas.

Fully Formed Futures

Identity begets purpose. When you begin to walk in who you truly are, you begin to find what you love and were created to do. Many of us are frustrated trying to find what we are to do, but we have not taken the time to find out who we are. Identity will always lead to destiny. It doesn't work the other way. If you seek your destiny before your identity, you will get lost in the process. Even if you find where you want to be, you will lack the fulfillment that comes from knowing who you are. Remember, identity is a fertile ground for destiny to bloom. This is why fostering a healthy identity from childhood produces so much fruit. You are essentially tilling the ground so that their future can take root and fully form.

It is our job to partner with the dreams that begin to spring up and to let them know they can accomplish what they put their heart to. Adaiah loves art. She enjoys to draw and create. She loves what she calls "fashion art"—creating clothes and trends. She will spend hours drawing outfits and deciding the right shoes and jewelry to go with them. My mother is a fantastic seamstress and when Adie started really connecting to this passion, I asked if she wanted to begin to make this dream real. She was so excited to learn to make fashion art. I don't know where the creativity that is in her will ultimately lead, but I want to honor where she is today and give her a place to begin to define it.

One of the reasons that many of us as adults have struggled with knowing our purpose is because we have never attempted to go after what is in our hearts. We are either too afraid of the risk, or are entirely oblivious to what we want to do. I desire to create spaces for my children, even at their early age, to begin to risk chasing the things that spring up from them knowing their identity.

To raise adults who can live free and chase their dreams requires honoring them as children and giving them the space to examine what will bloom in their field. Choose to partner with what you find. Choose to parent each child personally and individually, and they will not depart from the path that the Lord set for them.

CHAPTER NINE

PRESENTING JESUS

How do you talk to your children about Jesus? You love Him. You serve Him. You have dedicated your life to Him. Because He is so important to you and such a significant part of who you are, talking about Him to your children can be daunting. You don't want to mess this up. How do you share an intangible God with small children who cannot yet grasp the abstract? How do you present God to your children?

First, let's remove some of the pressure. Most of us want our children to grow up and know Jesus and to serve Him, but to carry the burden of making it happen isn't our responsibility. It is our job to teach and lead, but it is never our responsibility to save them, in fact you couldn't if you tried. Only Jesus can save. So take the pressure off of your shoulders. It is your job to present Jesus the way that He is. It is the Holy Spirit's job to draw them to Jesus. Do your job and let the Holy Spirit do His.

One of the fears we face is presenting Jesus incorrectly. When we start speaking about Him and encountering Him with our children, the enemy doesn't like it. He will try to make you insecure about where you are with Jesus. He will lie to you about how good of a job you are doing. He will accuse you of messing things up. But the good news is that if the enemy is trying to shut you up, you are on the right track. Don't let him! Take your thoughts captive and continue to move forward.

When I was struggling with if I was doing it "right," The Lord told me that He was more powerful than both my mistakes and my bad theology. I know this seems like a given, but when you are pressing in and giving your heart to your children for the sake of their encounters with Jesus, mess-ups feel bigger. My worry would kick in and run away with the possible negative effects of presenting God inaccurately. I took solace in knowing that my God desires to be in connection with my kiddos more than I desire them to know Him. His desire and pursuit is the ultimate, not my teaching. Jesus takes what I offer and has this miraculous way of weaving everything together for the good of my family. This is why co-laboring with Him is so wonderful.

You Are More Than Enough

Throw off whatever has been holding you back from presenting the God you know. You are equipped to present Jesus. You have the Holy Spirit living inside of you, the very Spirit that raised Christ from the dead. You have access to creative ways to present spiritual concepts because the mind of Christ has been given to you. You have everything you need for life and godliness, and this includes being equipped for equipping your children.

I want to share how I was convicted to talk about Jesus with my kids. This is by no means the only way to do so. For far too long, we have avoided talking about this subject with other parents, fearful of either feeling inadequate or coming across as a know-it-all. I desire to help open the topic and begin to learn from each other. If in reading about how I have been convicted to parent spiritual matters helps you, that's great. You can follow my lead, or create your own path. This section is intended to spur your creative thoughts about presenting Jesus to your young children.

The greatest conviction my husband and I share is that we want our children to know and encounter Christ's character. We want our children to be familiar with His goodness. We want them to not just know Jesus loves them, but we want them to feel it. We want them to understand God's mercy and grace. We desire them to encounter Jesus and His love so that the knowledge which follows brings revelation and life. When knowledge comes without encounter, we can fall prey to religion, doing the right things without connection in our heart. As a family, we want to build a springboard of encounter so that when deeper understanding and knowledge comes, it catapults them into a more sincere relationship with God.

Bigger Than Bible Stories

Practically speaking, this means we have chosen to focus more on His character and presence than just knowledge (Bible stories) at this point in their young lives. We desire for them to hunger and thirst for Him. When people truly get acquainted with who He is, they want to get to know Him. We know that Jesus lives today. He is not dead. He is risen. We want to speak about Him in a way that presents a living God. Kids love stories, but how you present them matters. We have chosen to tell living stories. Think about the way you tell your kids stories about how you met your spouse or about their grandparents. They are living stories. They are stories about people they know and love. We choose to present Jesus the same way. We do not read the Bible as a mere historical account. We talk about Jesus in living stories.

I value reading the Bible with my children. I want them to see that what we stand on as a family doesn't just come from our personal thoughts about life, but that it is backed by the Word of God. We love the Jesus Storybook Bible. It gives the stories of the Bible, but also refers to the fulfillment that came with Jesus.

I look for teachable moments with my children— ways to teach them as life is going on.

I look for teachable moments with my children. I look for ways to teach them as life is going on. When they are sick, we talk about how Jesus heals the sick. We talk about how Jesus said He came for those who were in need of a physician. We talk about how Jesus wants to heal us. We pray and expect Jesus to be who He said He was. Because we ask in faith, we receive and my family gets to experience His character and presence in reality.

If you look for teachable moments, you will be surprised by how many you find. I am purposeful about bringing Jesus into the conversation. We talk about what He loves to do, not just what He did. We leave room for Him to engage us in everyday life.

We talk about His goodness regularly. We talk about His kindness often. When bad things happen, we talk about how Jesus wants to work in the situation. He is not the author of the bad, but He is so incredible at turning bad things good, that He often gets credit for them. This is in essence, redemption. Explain it to them. Bring your children into your process. Don't hide your true emotions and pain from them. Show them how you walk out your maturity with Jesus. Show them how His redemption works in you and for you.

Children are naturally inquisitive. They have questions, lots of them. Don't be afraid of their questions. You don't have to know all the answers. Be honest about the fact that you are still learning. Keep the door open to talk about not just the good, but also the difficult.

Experiencing God For Themselves

It takes only one personal encounter with His goodness for us to know it is true. Don't rob your children of experiencing redemption and goodness in their lives. Don't fix their problems. Take them to Jesus and let Him work with you and your child to bring goodness and redemption to something that is important to them. Allow opportunities for their testimony to be developed while they are still young.

Adaiah's school teacher was using a behavior tool called the secret student. If the secret student had obeyed that day, then they got a prize out of the jar at the end of class. Adaiah really wanted to be the secret student. She would get in the car every day and tell me who the secret student was. She was so disappointed when week after week she wasn't the secret student. She began to believe that she would never be the secret student. We were having to focus our "I Am Statements" on feeling seen. I could have easily called the teacher and asked why they were on round two of the secret student and ask why Adie had not been chosen yet. I could have fixed it, but I would have robbed her of feeling seen by the Lord. We began to pray.

We asked Jesus to show Himself strong on her behalf. We asked for Adie to be the secret student. As a parent, this is scary. When you put God on the line for something that is important to your child, the places where you lack faith come to the surface.

When you put God on the line for something that is important to your child, the places where you lack faith come to the surface.

The first time we prayed, she came back into the car, almost in tears, and said, "It didn't happen. I wasn't the secret student." I reassured her that Jesus sees her. Instead of pulling back, we pressed in and we spent more time with Jesus asking Him to move on her behalf. The next day, she came running into the car, filled with joy. She had been the secret student! Adie came in so excited and exclaimed, "Mom! Jesus really does see me! You're right ... He is good to me!"

Adie didn't burst into the car to show me her treat, she couldn't wait to tell me what Jesus had done for her. It was a moment filled with such blessing for me, my heart nearly burst with His goodness for my child. Personally encountering His goodness is important. Lay down your fears and walk your children into the opportunity to encounter Him.

Children were given vast imaginations by the Lord. They love to create with their minds. They love to engage the unseen. Don't squash it. It is God-given. This is the part of my life that as an adult I have had to reawaken to encounter heaven. In Matthew 18, we are instructed to be like little children to enter the kingdom of heaven. Learn to feel comfortable in the place called imagination. If it is submitted to Jesus, it is a powerful tool to encounter Him.

Making the Spiritual Natural

We picture Jesus in our everyday life. We use the eyes of our heart to sense His Spirit. We practice this and make it fun. When we feel that Jesus wants to do something in our midst, we take the time to envision Him actually doing it. Children understand pictures and imagination, but putting words to what you mean can be difficult. Frame imagination in a way that makes sense to them. We choose to use the description of "the movie in our mind" to see Jesus at work.

We take the time to ask Jesus what He thinks about our choices. Most importantly, we take the time to listen. He is a living God. He doesn't speak only to adults, but also to children. Learning to hear and know His voice is possible even as a child. My kids first expected to hear Jesus like they hear me talk. We had to explain that we listen with our hearts, not just our ears. I encourage you to practice this with them with no pressure. Hebrews 5 says that by reason of use we exercise our spiritual senses. I want to use mine. I want my children to use theirs. We practice hearing, feeling, and seeing God. I have purposed to take the spiritual and make it natural.

So is it okay for parents to lead their own children to Jesus? Certainly. For centuries, it has been the stories and testimonies of the family that have brought new generations to Jesus. There are many times in the Old Testament where we are instructed to speak of His good works and to talk of Him to our children and our children's children. It is not manipulation to speak of what you know to be truth. In fact, it is your responsibility.

When we began to talk about the cross, we spoke plainly about what Jesus did. Jesus came to set us free, to make us clean. Jesus came to restore connection with us. Jesus came to give us life, and life that is full. Jesus came to make things right in our hearts, and in this world. Jesus came to empower us to live like He did.

We desire our children to find Jesus for who He is and what He does, not out of fear of going to hell. We choose our language carefully so we won't promote a fear-based relationship with God. Fear is the opposite of love and faith. We desire that the foundation of faith they build on be based upon the reality of who Jesus is, not the fear of what could happen to them if they don't choose him. Fear may be a sufficient motivator to force a decision, but it will never motivate to intimacy. It is the heart of the Father that we are after, and fear will never lead you to intimacy with His heart.

When we bring up sin, we do so in light of who Jesus is. Jesus is so good that He can't be in connection with us with our sin in us and on us. But because He is so good, He made a way for us to clean off all of our "yucky." What happened on the cross was that Jesus chose to put all of our yucky (our sin) on Him so that we have the opportunity to be clean.

Present Jesus, Let Them Choose

We chose not to force our children to pray "the prayer." That is their choice, but it is our job to present Jesus. Where Jesus is lifted high, He will draw all men to Himself. When you are faithful to present Jesus, He is faithful to work on their hearts. There has been a moment in each of our children's lives where they have understood and wanted to accept what Jesus offers. They were already acquainted with Him because He was already a part of our everyday lives. It was a very easy step for each of them because they knew His character and His goodness.

Each story of my children first choosing Jesus is a treasure. Some jewel stones are so valuable that they are gathered for only those who are closest to you. For those of you who wonder about your young ones understanding the fullness of what the cross accomplished, I want to breathe peace into you. Jesus very pointedly told me how He takes even the smallest commitment and works with it. Just look at the man hanging besides Jesus on the cross. Salvation is the start of choosing. It is not the end, it is the beginning. Walking with Jesus requires a continual choosing, for us and for them.

Once our children had Jesus in their hearts, we taught them they also had the Holy Spirit living inside them. We use our imagination and envision Him inside of us. Sometimes He is working on our hearts, bandaging our "owies." Sometimes He is surging through our bodies like a glorious golden presence. We practice releasing this golden presence upon others. When we pray, we imagine that presence going through our hand and filling up the person we are praying for. We make the supernatural practical.

One of my favorite pictures the Holy Spirit gave us was when He showed us that He was making each of us into a big tree—tall and strong. We pictured fruit growing from our arms. We talked about the fruit of the Spirit and how without the Holy Spirit we can't expect to grow the fruit like those mentioned in Galatians. We used the movie in our mind to watch our fruit grow big and juicy.

This picture reminded me of something I once heard that has become a clear way to set my expectation for my children. How many of us have been out and about shopping and have seen a kid just having a tantrum? It's probably happened to you at some time. I've watched as people have murmured, "Control your child." Those bystanders miss the point. Parenting is not about controlling your child. Parenting is about teaching your child to control themselves. We train them, but it is their responsibility. You can teach a child to manage themselves, but self-control is clearly stated as a fruit of the Spirit. Until they have the Holy Spirit coursing through their veins, self-control is only something you can teach in principle. True self-control comes from being connected to the Holy Spirit and letting Him work in your life. Give your children grace to grow fruit, and don't expect fruit that they can't produce.

Partner With the Holy Spirit

When your children have Jesus in their heart, how you parent changes. You get to partner with the Holy Spirit inside of them. It is the Spirit that will lead them into all truth. Don't take your greatest parenting ally out of the picture. Work with Him in presenting Jesus. After all, the Holy Spirit is part of the Trinity. Raise your kids to understand that it is His kindness that leads to repentance; it is His voice that gently convicts, never condemns. When you do this, your kids become acquainted with His movings while their spirits are still tender and pliable. They will know the way He speaks, regardless of where they are later in life.

We have chosen not to avoid the fact that we are in a battle and that there is good and bad. We talk to our children about how there is someone who doesn't want them to connect to Jesus and that he is consciously trying to keep them from living full like Jesus. We focus on the fact that we have the choice to align with Jesus or not. Jesus defeated the enemy, but the enemy wants to keep us from choosing life. He lurks to kill, steal, and destroy the life Jesus has for us.

We have chosen not to avoid the fact that we are in a battle and that there is good and bad.

One time Kai asked me if the enemy had real power. We had just watched the Avengers, and as most little boys, Kai loves super heroes. The Lord gave me an analogy to answer him. There is a scene in the movie where the Hulk takes Lokie and whacks him back and forth like a rag doll. I told Kai that the enemy did have power, but when God was ready, He could take the enemy and end the battle just like the Hulk did. The enemy does have power, but it pales in comparison to the power of God. Jesus truly is the ultimate superhero. He rendered the enemy defeated on the cross, and He works with us and through us to allocate that defeat every day.

Whether or not you choose to present Jesus the way that I do, the take away is to be intentional about presenting Jesus. You are creating a foundation in their life that is built on the character and presence of Jesus. Regardless of the storms that come when they are older, the solid foundation will remain.

When doubts and questions come, they will have a history and a testimony of experience to fall back on. Create spaces where your kids can encounter heaven, where the presence of God is tangible. Don't shy away from talking about your King. Make it fun and make it practical. When you work with the Father for the sake of your children, you will find yourself in moments of divine inspiration and divine connection, both with Him and with your family.

CHAPTER TEN

THEY REFLECT YOU

Parenting is one of life's most beautiful gifts. It brings some of your greatest moments, and it is a rewarding experience. It is full of joy, full of fulfillment, and full of fun. There are those precious moments when you look your child in the eyes and feel the deep connection that words really can't do justice. There are moments when you have battled through a lie and come out on the other side victorious. There are moments where time just seems to stand still as you watch your child. And there are moments in time you will never forget because you stopped to capture it in your heart.

But as any parent knows, parenting is not for the faint of heart. It is challenging. It is tough, and sometimes the hard times feel like they outweigh the good times. It is full of dirty diapers, late nights, lots of crying, and lots of sacrifice. It can be full of pain and even heartache. There are seasons where the responsibility seems to pile up higher than the laundry. There are days where you would do anything for a moment of silence and a shower.

These are the days when you recognize you are on the front lines fighting not just for your kids, but for yourself.

For most parents, it is easy to sacrifice for our kids. Our maternal/paternal nature kicks in and we lose ourselves in the day in and day out routine of parenting our kids. This is why you hear so many parenting gurus talk about taking time for yourself. It is simple, but true. When mom and dad aren't taken care of, the entire family unit suffers. The balance of knowing when to take a breather and when to keep at it can get harder to find the longer we serve, love, and bless our families. But if you don't keep your cup filled, then you will have nothing to pour out.

Whether a single parent or married, working a job or staying at home, we are all pushing in to raise kids that know and embrace their identity and know and embrace Jesus. One of the most destructive forces in parenting is insecurity—insecurity in who we are as parents and in our abilities. When we let insecurity mess with our heads and our hearts, we become crippled to respond with grace to our families and to each other. It is no secret that some of the most vicious places to get emotionally torn down are with other moms. When insecurity runs rampant, it is easy to criticize and judge other parents. We cut each other down about our weaknesses instead of building each other up. We judge parents whose kids misbehave. We judge parents who do things differently than us. We judge parents who do things "worse" than us, and we judge parents who do things "better" than us. All of this is done to create a false sense of security about our own parenting style.

What we align with is a choice. I am blatantly asking you to choose today to lay down judgment. I am asking you to lay down insecurity. It is not healthy and it is definitely not helpful. It does not promote you connecting to other parents, and it does not cause you to become the parent you want to be.

Shedding Shame

Our goal is to be healthy and whole in the way we respond to our children. We have to rid ourselves of the issues that plague us and keep us from choosing this. One such issue is shame. Shame is a painful feeling of humiliation or distress that covers us when we become conscious of wrong or foolish behavior on our part. Shame can easily attach itself to us. When we get angry for no reason. When we yell. When we are too busy. When we just don't have the energy to engage. No matter what causes it, shame is debilitating. It keeps you paralyzed in your mistake and it shuts out the mercy and grace Jesus wants to extend to you. Shame will keep you from pressing into your children. It will ultimately keep you disconnected and isolated.

I am asking you to throw off shame. Put your trust in Jesus. Receive His grace for your mistakes, and then pick yourself up and go forward with confidence. Those that believe in Him will not be put to shame (Romans 10). We can get trapped in our failures, unable to achieve the things we desire. Receive His provision for forgiveness. Receive what He accomplished on the cross. Accept His grace and then move forward without beating yourself up.

The enemy is cunning and is gunning to take you out. When you give way to what he says about you, you will succumb to the onslaught of shame. There will be times when words, situations, and even people speak negatively about you. There is a way to rise above that attack. Find the courage to go and ask Jesus how He feels about you. There is nothing that dispels the lies faster than the truth. Be willing to cast off the fear and shame and go sit with Jesus. That is the place of victory. That is the place of overcoming. We do not have to convince or condition ourselves to think with confidence. We walk with confidence when we hear how Jesus feels about us. He makes it easy. We overcome because He overcame for us.

When issues manifest, they are designed to bring up your brokenness. It is sovereignly orchestrated to bring your un-healed places to the surface. This is actually a gift from the Lord. When these issues arise, there is a grace to deal with them so they no longer define us. There are places in our hearts that are only accessed by those closest to us. Those are the ones the Lord uses to sharpen and refine us to look like Him. Many times our children are the piece of flint used to sharpen us. Through parenting, we have the opportunity to heal our own heart's wounds.

Loud Actions, Soft Words

One of the hardest realities to face in parenting is that our actions speak louder than our words. You impart into your children who you are, not just what you say. As a simple example, if you continually tell your children that you love them, but then resort to abuse to control them, they will not pick up the love you confess. I know this example is extreme, but I am making a point. Children see through the facades we put up. They see who people really are. They hear their words, but they watch their actions. As we purposefully parent, we must remain aware that if we want our children to receive what we say, then we must live it.

We must become genuine in the way we live. We must walk out our identity in confidence if we expect our children to do the same. The saying, "Do what I say and not what I do," is not applicable. It does not work. Children need their parents to be real, genuine, and authentic. They need us to embrace our God-given identity. They need us to walk, trusting Jesus with our insecurities. They need to see us overcome the lies of the enemy we face. They need to see our struggles, and they need to see us victorious. We don't sugar-coat things for our kids. We give them us, live and uncut—not finished and neatly packaged. We give them us, works in process.

While reading you may have realized that you were not parented with identity in mind. You may have realized that you don't have any "I Am Statements" for yourself. You may have realized that you were not blessed in your spirit. You may not feel received, accepted, and valid for who you are. The good news is that it is never too late to start receiving and walking free. Jesus truly loves talking to you about how He designed you to reflect Him. It is a matter of gaining the courage to begin to seek Jesus for your personal definition. Take the time to ask Jesus how He feels about you. Ask Him to tenderly speak to you about how He made you. He will talk ... be encouraged, and listen.

It is never too late to start receiving and walking free.

If you were not fortunate enough to grow up in a healthy family, I want to speak hope to you. You can have a redeemed and healthy family now. You are not subject to your past and you are not subject to your genealogy. Jesus loves to redeem and He loves family. You, with His help, can create a new legacy. A legacy of faith. A legacy of adventure. A legacy of love. A healthy family is not a pipe dream. Partner with Him, and it will become a reality.

Choose life for yourself and you choose life for your family. You are an adult now, but if these places were not parented into you, receive from the Father. Learn to rest as a son or daughter and learn to rest in His unashamed love for you. If there is a place lacking in your world, submit it to the cross, and watch as the Father gently parents health and truth into your spirit and into your soul. Allow yourself and your brokenness to be parented into health. You will become a more whole person, and a much better parent as a result.

Doorkeepers

As a parent you set the atmosphere for your household. You are the doorkeepers to your children. Just as we open doors for grace and peace to flow in our households, we can also open doors of destruction. When you are struggling with fear, you may find that your children also struggle with fear in their hearts. When you are aggravated internally, you will find that your children pick up on your restlessness and are more aggravated with each other. What you open, you open not just to yourself, but to them as well. When you are struggling with failure, your children may struggle with their performance.

Not every struggle that your children have is a result of one of your struggles, but if your children are struggling, it is a good idea to make sure you are aligned with Jesus. When you are out of alignment, you leave them vulnerable to be out of alignment as well. When you allow the enemy to speak to you, you leave the door open for him to speak to your family as well. Be diligent about keeping yourself aligned, and you will minimize where the enemy has access to your kiddos.

There was a season where my daughter Adie was having really tormenting dreams. They were waking her up several times a night, and it was wearing on her, and it was wearing on us. As we were seeking breakthrough for her, Paul and I both were convicted of opening up doors of fear. We were in a difficult transition as a family and both of us were personally dealing with our own fears about how the transition was going to work out. When we heard Jesus, Paul and I repented to the Lord, and then we went and asked Adie for forgiveness for allowing fear in the house. We prayed for peace and we all chose to trust Jesus and His protection of us. That night Adie slept the entire night and the tormenting nightmares stopped.

Ungodly beliefs are just what they state. They are beliefs that do not align with God's thoughts toward you or a situation. We all have places where we don't think like Jesus does. Part of becoming whole is taking those thoughts and laying them down at the feet of Jesus and letting Him minister to our hearts and minds. This is the process of renewing our mind. 2 Corinthians 10:5 says we should take every thought captive to make it obedient to Christ. Simply put, we need to check what we think to see if it matches what God thinks. When we become familiar with Jesus' character, we can identify where our thoughts don't match His. Many times we can spot them easier in other people's thought processes than we can in our own. This is why it is important to have friends who speak truth to you.

When you are parenting "I Am Statements" and when you are calling out the things that don't align with your children's identity, you are helping them identify their ungodly beliefs. We call them UGB's. When parenting draws out the ugly in you, be willing to deal with your UGB's.

The great thing about intentional parenting is that your children pick up the principles so quickly! Before you know it, you will be in a funk, speaking ill of yourself, and your child will say something to you about it. There have been times when my children will say, "Momma, don't receive that," or, "That's a UGB." When we train our children in truth, they know how to wield the sword of truth. When we parent our kid's identity, we can't be surprised when they walk in it. As a parent, it takes humility to be able to receive from them in your weakness, but one of the values we have is that every person in our family is powerful. Every one of us, regardless of age, has permission to be powerful for the sake of everyone's health. We have given our children permission to be part of our healing, just as we are a part of theirs.

We call each other up to our God-given identity. We call each other up in our character. We don't call out each other's sin. We don't point out mistakes to hurt. When we deal with sin, we do it in a way that draws each other to Jesus and draws us to want to embrace truth. 1 Corinthians 13:7 (NIV) says, "Love always protects, always trusts, always hopes, always perseveres." We call each other up, not out, because we love one another. Make love the cornerstone for your actions, and it won't be a problem. If you are about to parent out of frustration, step away, and regain access to the way Jesus feels about them; then you can parent in love, calling them into their real identity, calling them to Him.

Face Your Past to Free Your Family

As we press in towards our personal freedom we may realize we still have issues with our parents that need to be dealt with. What you put your faith in is what you produce. But when you put your faith in what they enemy may do (fear), you create the very outcome you were afraid of. So what you fear, you create. Let's look at someone who repetitively says, "I will never be like my mom. I will never control like she does." When you focus your vision on what you don't want, and when you fear becoming that reality, you actually promote that same behavior in you. You begin to control because what you look at is what you produce. What you sow is what you reap. When you sow judgment of an action, you very well may reap it.

It is important to recognize the dysfunction in our families. This is not so we can judge and remain in bitterness, but so we can look at the truth. The truth sets us free. If you have issues with your mom or dad, be willing to work with Jesus to get set free from those. It will probably not be an overnight testimony, but it will be worth whatever time it takes. As I have partnered with Jesus in parenting my children, I have had to face my own issues with my parents. I can honestly say that I am enjoying the fruit of dealing with my offenses, bitterness, and pain. I have a thriving relationship with my mom and dad. It's not perfect. We still have our frustrations, but we have learned to connect our hearts to each other despite them.

Look at your family line as a ladder. If you don't deal with the issues that go up the ladder, then those same issues will go down the ladder. Scripture says the sins or iniquities of the father go to the third and fourth generation. Our parents' disposition and problems become our pre-disposition. But the promise is that the blessings go on to a thousand generations (Exodus 20:5). When we are diligent to break our harmful family patterns, we create new realities for ourselves, our children, and even our parents.

When we are diligent to break our harmful family patterns, we create new realities for our families.

When I began breaking co-dependence in my heart towards my family, I was shocked at the waves this created in my other family members. I was looking towards the freedom that it would create for me and my babies, but it began to change my parents' reality as well. Me choosing healthy boundaries showed them what was possible, and it created a space for the Lord to talk to them about their issues with co-dependency as well. What you don't deal with goes down the ladder, but if you deal with your family patterns, freedom can go up and down the ladder.

I am not advocating that you put yourself in unhealthy situations as you deal with your family problems. I fully realize there are situations of abuse and the like, that are unhealthy to remain in. If you are in one of those, get out. However, even if it doesn't include continued relationship, getting your heart set free is of vital importance. Working forgiveness in and through your wounds will create a new reality for your generations. The Father is always so gentle when He restores and redeems. There should be no fear that He will parent you like them. His character is entirely good and entirely for you and your success. Take the time to work through your issues as you find them. Doing so will produce sweet treasures in your heart and freedom for you and your family.

Break The Cycle of Dysfunction

There are things we have done, sometimes unknowingly, that are unhealthy for us and for our kids. One place that is true is with our dreams. We have stunted our dreams for the sake of raising our kids well. Women in particular have a problem with aborting their dreams. This is a cycle of dysfunction that many of us are guilty of. When we were young, we knew we had a purpose, a destiny, something that we could contribute ... but when we became parents and took on the weight of responsibility that it carries, many of us laid down those dreams.

Being a parent has always been something that I wanted, but I struggled immensely in losing myself in the process. Putting your entire heart into loving your kids is admirable, but you still have a call to love on those outside your family. There are things we dreamed of that seem impossible to attain while our children are young, and some of them do need to be delayed until a later time. But, when we set our dreams down altogether, we are, in essence, setting down a part of ourselves.

It is a cycle. Whether we have been parented with our destiny and passions in mind or not, all of us have felt the nagging of our heart and its pull to something of eternal significance. We begin to identify it, and then we have children. The zeal of our youth fades into the mundane ins and outs of caring for our babies. We lay down those dreams and aspirations while at the same time teaching our children that they were made special, with something that only they can offer the world. They engage it right up until the cycle touches them and they have to choose if they are going to lay down their dreams to raise their children so those children can accomplish theirs.

The cycle is disorienting and dysfunctional. It clothes itself in good intentions and creates a false sense of nobility. It is not noble to sacrifice your identity on this altar and function in opposition to who God designed you to be. We are teaching our children to embrace and walk in their identity, so shouldn't we do the same?

"Wait a minute!" I just heard you say, "Are you advocating that we push our children aside to go after our own heart's desires and ambitions?" Of course not. The process of laying down your heart is usually not a quick switch, it is a slow erosion, and it happens without us even knowing. We are so accustomed to giving, we begin to lose acquaintance with our own desires. We may even feel the yearning of our hearts, but if it has been shut down for too long, we don't even know where to begin to turn it back on. We need to find out if we have hidden our desires underneath our parenting because we are fearful. Are we hiding because we don't believe in our own calling and capabilities? Are we fearful of embracing success? Are we giving ourselves excuses not to be set free? What we long for is the balance of walking in identity and parenting identity.

We impart into our children who we are. They learn from our lives. If we have stopped pursuing what is in our hearts, what are we actually teaching them? Are they believing they can accomplish what is in their hearts? Your example is leading the way. The best way to teach them this is to show them.

Your dream doesn't have to be world-changing and enormous, but it does have to be your dream. When there is something that connects to your heart and you share the pursuit of it with your children, THEN you are not only teaching them, but showing them that they can accomplish their goals. You are building a history with them that will speak louder than the doubt and the "I can't."

I share my dreams with my kids even while they are young. I talk to them about what Jesus is telling me. We pray together about my desires, and then when those prayers are answered, we rejoice together. I don't hide my struggles in partnering with God, and I don't hide my fears. I may simplify them so they can understand, but I remain open. If they have questions, I answer them. I don't push it upon them, but I am open. It is my dream, not theirs. I just share my journey with them. In doing so, I am creating a testimony that God will partner with me. I am building a history of victory and accomplishment. I am showing them that what is in their heart is possible to achieve. We impart who we are, not what we say. When you live your dreams, you have added weight to the words you speak over theirs.

I am building a history of victory and accomplishment. I am showing them what is in their heart is possible to achieve.

Stop the cycle. Purpose to reopen the wells of your heart that have been capped as you embraced parenting. Engage your dreams at the same time you engage theirs.

Live the Dream Now!

Adaiah loves art. In school she started learning about books, authors, and illustrators and was intrigued. She came home talking about wanting to "someday" have a book that she illustrated. "Why can't you do it now?" I asked. "Why does it have to be 'someday?'"

She liked the idea of pushing into it. Someday is today, so we have started on the project. We are in process of her story, and she is creating the pictures she wants to accompany her pages. I want to partner with her heart now, not just when she comes of age. I want to teach her that her ideas have weight, and that they can go from an idea to reality ... even now. I want to walk with her through the mental battles that arise when we embrace our own creativity for others to see. I want her to feel safe to step out and learn that she can do it. Can I partner with her without pursuing my passions? Sure. But the chances of them pursuing their dreams becoming a way of life are a lot higher if they see me practice what I preach. I want my kids to run their race with perseverance and hope that they can live fully alive, fully free, accomplishing what's in their heart ... in every stage of life.

You give love when you know that you are loved. You instill identity when you know and walk in your own. You give peace when you have peace. You teach overcoming power when you know the overcoming power of Jesus in your own life. It all comes down to maintaining a thriving relationship with Jesus. He will keep your heart filled with love when the days are long, and the things that pull on your time, energy and strength are more than you think you can handle. He will truly be your anchor and your hope.

We are a part of the family of heaven. We are adopted into His family and we call Him, Abba, Daddy. He parents us with a heart that is slow to anger and abounding in love. He will guide you through the sticky places in your parenting if you let Him. Embrace Him. Embrace His Spirit. Embrace this journey and walk forward in confidence imparting identity. Let His imprint be clearly shown in your children.

RECOMMENDATIONS

Although there are plenty of great resources on parenting, these are a few of my favorite.

LOVING OUR KIDS ON PURPOSE:
MAKING A HEART-TO-HEART CONNECTION

by Danny Silk

You CAN raise good kids! Loving Our Kids on Purpose combines the principles of the Kingdom of God and revival to form a powerful strategy for parents. *"Where the Spirit of the Lord is there is freedom"* (2 Corinthians 3:17). Rather than the traditional approaches that train children to learn to accept being controlled by well-meaning parents and adults, this book teaches parents how to train children to manage their freedoms and protect their important heart-to-heart relationships.

Children were designed with the core need of freedom. To deny this or live ignorant of it eventually destroys the trust connection between parent and child. *"There is no fear in love; but perfect love casts out fear, because fear involves torment. But he who fears has not been made perfect in love"* (1 John 4:18 NKJV). *Loving Our Kids on Purpose* introduces paradigms, perceptions, skills, and ideas that will help parents reduce fear by eliminating the tool of punishment and strengthening the core character of their children by empowering their self-control and value for their relationship with their parents.

Available at www.lovingonpurpose.com
Also at www.amazon.com

PARENTING WITH LOVE AND LOGIC

by Foster Cline and Jim Fay

This parenting book shows you how to raise self-confident, motivated children who are ready for the real world. Learn how to parent effectively while teaching your children responsibility and growing their character.

Establish healthy control through easy-to-implement steps without anger, threats, nagging, or power struggles.

Available at www.loveandlogic.com
Also at www.amazon.com

LOVE AND LOGIC MAGIC FOR EARLY CHILDHOOD: PRACTICAL PARENTING FROM BIRTH TO SIX YEARS

by Jim Fay and Charles Fay Ph.D.

Parenting little ones can be exhausting...until you discover Love and Logic. Take the exhaustion out and put the fun into parenting your little one. This book is for you If you want help with:

- ❖ potty training,
- ❖ temper tantrums,
- ❖ bedtime,
- ❖ whining,
- ❖ time-out
- ❖ hassle-free mornings,
- ❖ and many other every day challenges!

This book is the tool parents of little ones have been waiting for. America's Parenting Experts Jim and Charles Fay, Ph.D., help you start your child off on the right foot. The tools in Love and Logic Magic for Early Childhood will give you the building blocks you need to create children who grow up to be responsible, successful teens and adults. And as a bonus you will enjoy every stage of your child's life and look forward to sharing a lifetime of joy with them.

Available at www.loveandlogic.com
Also at www.amazon.com

FOR THIS CHILD I PRAY

CD by Tanya Crump

This CD offers parents and caregivers of children the necessary and vital tools to join the journey of praying for their children. Using a harp and bowl (prayers joined with music), it teaches parents to pray scriptures and truth over their children through the art of music. Specifically, it is prayers created directly from the scriptures recorded over traditional hymns and lullabies.

"He will gather the lambs in His arms, and carry them in His bosom, and gently lead those who are with young" (Isaiah 40:11). As you listen to the CD and pray over your children you will feel your Heavenly Father bringing peace and comfort as He carries your child close to His heart.

Available at tanyacrump.com
Also at www.cdbaby.com and on iTunes

THE JESUS STORYBOOK BIBLE: EVERY STORY WHISPERS HIS NAME

by Sally Lloyd-Jones

The Moonbeam Award Gold Medal Winner in the religion category, *The Jesus Storybook Bible* tells the Story beneath all the stories in the Bible. At the center of the Story is a baby, the child upon whom everything will depend. Every story whispers His name. From Noah to Moses to the great King David—every story points to Him. He is like the missing piece in a puzzle—the piece that makes all the other pieces fit together.

Available at amazon.com

MEET TAI ANN

Tai Ann McClendon lives life full, free, and fun! She believes in a limitless God and expects big things for herself and her family. For Tai Ann, identity is foundational to all other experiences. Knowing who you are lets you walk with confidence because you believe God will do everything He says He will do!

Tai Ann is committed to pressing into the favor of God for breakthrough—for miracles, strategy, and solutions—for individuals as well as for businesses. She believes that walking in timing and partnering with the supernatural always provides positive results.

Tai Ann travels extensively and relishes the discovery of people, places, and cultures. She is passionate about catching someone's true identity (who they really are) and discovering what God is about to do in their life.

A native Texan, Tai Ann and her husband, Paul, have been happily married for more than eleven years. Together they have three children: Adaiah, Kai, and Zoe. Tai Ann is determined to help each of them live an amazing life—beyond the mundane and filled with joy and blessing.

TO INVITE TAI ANN TO SPEAK, VISIT WWW.TAIANN.TV

TAI ANN & PAUL

KAI, PAUL
ZOE, ADAIAH, TAI ANN

WWW.TAIANN.TV